ZOMBIE PROUST

by

Jérôme Prieur

*Translated from the French
by Nancy Kline*

Les Fugitives
London

This first English-language edition published by Les Fugitives editions in the United Kingdom in July 2025 • Les Fugitives Ltd, 91 Cholmley Gardens, Fortune Green Road, London NW6 1UN • www.lesfugitives.com • Originally published as *Proust fantôme* © Éditions Gallimard, 2001 • English-language translation © Nancy Kline, 2025 • All cited excerpts from French works translated by Nancy Kline • Cover design by Dominic Lee • Cover artwork by Rafail Kordelas • Text design by MacGuru Ltd • All rights reserved • No part of this publication may be reproduced, stored in a retrieval system or transmitted in any form or by any means, electronic, mechanical, photocopying, recording or otherwise, without prior permission in writing from the Publishers • A CIP catalogue record for this book is available from the British Library • The rights of Jérôme Prieur to be identified as author, and the rights of Nancy Kline to be identified as translator of this work have been identified in accordance with Section 77 of the Copyright, Designs and Patents Act 1988 • Printed in the UK by CMP • EU Authorised Representative: Easy Access System Europe - Mustamäe tee 50, 10621 Tallinn, Estonia, gpsr.requests@easproject.com • ISBN: 978-1-0683001-2-7 • Cet ouvrage a bénéficié du soutien du Programme d'aide à la publication de l'Institut français et du Centre National du Livre •

Praise for *Proust fantôme*

'Prieur has succeeded magnificently in bringing his portrait of Proust to life.' – ***Le Monde***

'Prieur explores places, questions traces, lingers on moments of Proust's life, sentences from *In Search of Lost Time*, images – again and again – like those words, haloed in mystery, which open wide the doors of imagination.' – ***Télérama***

'Every page is shot through with the feeling of overwhelming, enthusiastic, affectionate gratitude that readers of *In Search of Lost Time* feel for Proust the writer and Proust the man.' – ***Le Matricule des anges***

'Scarcely any other book on Proust evades with such effortless skill the classic dilemma of whether to relate everything to the work or to the man. Prieur resurrects them both as a single phantom, in the nighttime favoured by Proust, perfectly conjuring up scents and tastes, with a love which owes nothing to neurosis.' – ***Journal du Dimanche***

Contents

Boulevard Haussmann	1
His Eyes	4
Portrait from Memory	5
Roman à clefs	7
Still Alive	9
Paris-Prague	12
Imaginary Lives	13
The Visible Body	16
Deep-Sea Diver	17
Dead City	20
In the Shop Window	22
Returning	23
'Monsieur Proust is dead!'	24
The Mummy	25
Likeness	26
His Mark	28
Sacha Guitry	29
The Birdman	32
Those of Our Land	33
Cabourg, 1914	37
His Voice	38
Waves from the Past	39
Scents	42

Cinematograph	44
The End of the World	47
November 1922	49
Funeral Procession	50
At Père-Lachaise	51
Mausoleums	53
The Registry Office	55
The Image of his Mother	58
Reincarnations	59
Prowler	61
Theory of Ghosts	62
A Family Photograph	64
Faces	68
Ex-voto	71
Immense Rebus	74
Trophies	75
Glacial Cold	77
Gliding Like an Ice Skater	78
Fit of Laughter	80
Everything Interests Him	83
The News	85
One O'clock in the Morning	87
Unpredictable	89
Out of Time	90
False Dandy	92
It's Temporary	94
The Bedroom	95

At the Theatre	97
Hallucination	99
The Paper Bed	100
Vigil	101
The Flood of Portraitists	102
The Reader's Way	105
Interior, Woman Reading	106
From Morning to Evening	108
Céleste Appears	109
Flesh and Blood	111
Day and Night	115
Pierrot	117
Replacement	119
The Invisible Man	120
Expeditions	122
Unfathomed Depths	124
Last Outings	125
Incorporeal	126
The Mist of Fumigations	128
Untouchable	130
Tomorrow	132
Alive	133
Bookshelf	136
Acknowledgments	138

Editor's note

Given that there exist multiple English translations of the titles of Proust's books, and also to preserve the author's use of *La Recherche* as an abbreviated title – which is widely understood in French to imply an affinity and familiarity with *À la recherche du temps perdu*, and which has no equivalent in English – we have elected to keep Proust's French titles. Books written by other French authors have had their titles translated into English.

ZOMBIE PROUST

To Thierry Thomas
To Jacques Laurens

The present writes out words before us, but what our future will make of them we cannot know until later. And a chain extends through all our existence linking what is already dead to what is full of life.

Marcel Proust, *Found Texts*

Boulevard Haussmann

First, you have to wait, in the lobby of the commercial bank that currently occupies 102 Boulevard Haussmann, as if you had come to take care of an overdraft or discuss an investment. Thursdays only, after lunch. Five or six people gather with the air of co-conspirators ignoring each other.

The hostess has distributed a brochure, to bring us up to speed. The pockmarked American sunk in the seat beside me abruptly points at a name, not knowing how to read it, afraid of making a mistake. I emphasize the last syllable. *Quiou.* I repeat it, deliberately. *Kew.* Robert de Montesquiou. The Texan nods, reassured, and goes back to underlining all the phrases he reckons are essential.

We finally ascend to the first floor, led by a young lady. The landing is one station of a pilgrimage: it is *here* that Proust wrote *La Recherche*, it is *here* that he came to live after the death of his *maman*; she knew the building because this is where his aunt lived. The young lady repeats the word '*maman*' several times. Proust's *maman*. You feel almost a part of the family. We move into the hall, which used to belong to the building next door. The girl explains that Proust never left his bed. She talks in a loud voice. It is here that he found inspiration. Thus he carefully chose this apartment, though it was neither far from the noise nor the chestnut trees on the boulevard nor the dust of the city, halfway between the Place Saint-Antoine and the Saint-Lazare railway station.

Then, we push open the door.

We enter the room.

The bedroom walls are covered in cork, but the spaces between windows are lined with simple ornamental wallpaper. The layer of bark which once cloaked this living space from top to bottom, walls and ceiling, went untreated. You would have thought you were inside a wine cork: it was a grotto, a quarry entirely blackened by fumigations. The idea came from his friend Anna de Noailles, who got it from Henry Bernstein. She had recommended this arrangement to make Proust's den airtight, to seal it off from the world. In the apartment above, an American dentist had installed his office – it was the heroic era of the dentist's drill – and he had even seen fit to marry a musician, a harpist.

The original furnishings are gone, several to the Carnavalet Museum: the copper bed, the nightstands, the armchair. The portrait of Proust by Jacques-Émile Blanche is just an enlarged photograph, even more insipid in black and white, despite the camellia. In the great wood-paneled salon, today the boardroom, everything has disappeared except the chevron parquet flooring, which is 'of the period.' The young lady emphasizes this point.

From the landing, where the lift already existed, though it was a different model, you can glimpse the passageway that led to Céleste, his housekeeper, his maid, his nurse, his paid companion. And its peephole, which allowed her to monitor, as though they were funds being moved, the comings and goings of her master, the look of his visitors, especially when they were too-heavily-perfumed women.

Another lady from the bank has joined our little troop, she keeps an eye on the proceedings, acquiesces, adds a detail. Our young guide is new to the job. Without her supervisor, she might have forgotten the most important thing: to open, near the white marble mantelpiece (the original), a drawer in the bureau (no longer Proust's bureau), and to take out a willow basket from which to distribute *petites madeleines*, each one wrapped up in its own little cellophane pouch.

His Eyes

It seems he saw everything without your being aware of it, noticed the slightest detail, recorded nonstop. He was better than a camera, Céleste reports in her memoirs. With him, as everyone agreed after his death, pretense was impossible, you were searched out by a spotlight, seen through, radiographed, 'X-rayed.'

There was something unique about his eyes, like a 'recording device' which let nothing escape. A thousand-faceted gaze like that of a fly, the gaze of a magnifying glass, enlarging everything it focuses on.

His body seemed literally to adhere to furniture, fabrics, knick-knacks. 'Through all the pores of his skin,' comments Ramon Fernandez, 'he seemed to inhale every bit of the reality contained in his bedroom, in the instant, in me, and the kind of ecstasy that suffused his face was exactly that of the medium who receives the invisible messages of things.' Jacques Rivière recalls the electricity, the overvoltage of sensations. Before Proust, you were haloed, hallowed. Under the spell of his voice, the physical sensation was of being plunged into a bath of pure sensitivity, of suddenly being transported into another world, of being irradiated.

Portrait from Memory

In the early Sixties, in Roger Stéphane's televised *Portrait from Memory* of Proust, Jean Cocteau recited his pearls as though inspired, his camel hair coat draped casually over his shoulders. He considered that the Verdurins were really 'very New Wave' and that Marcel's handwriting in his correspondence was as hard to work out as a walnut from its shell. Paul Morand and the Princess Soutzo took their turns, and then François Mauriac, Madame André Maurois, the Duke de Gramont, Philippe Soupault, the Marquis de Lauris, Jacques de Lacretelle, Daniel Halévy, Emmanuel Berl, who related that Proust threw his bedroom slippers in Berl's face because Proust thought him 'stupid' and wanted to persuade him that the only thing of importance in life is knowing how to be alone in the world (whereas the young man obstinately refused to separate from his fiancée!). As for the most moving of them all, Céleste Albaret literally relived, on the verge of tears, the last instants of Monsieur Proust's life, his death in the apartment on Rue Hamelin.

The survivors assembled for this television program were witnesses at a wake, but more than that, they were forlorn relics, abandoned by Proust's oeuvre itself, like pieces of wreckage washed up on the shore. To them might easily have been added some of the formerly young men employed as personal secretaries for the book, were it not that in Proust's era his open secret could not be discussed in a public forum – the 'affliction' that he had studied in himself, without its being possible to go further. It was not to be talked about, 'but you know what I'm alluding to,' simpered Mauriac, in his cracked voice, staring into the camera.

Roman à clefs

We find it hard to imagine now, at such a distance, but reading *La Recherche* was originally a party game (Robert de Montesquiou died of it, they say, when he felt himself too exposed, too much on display in the book). The most well-intentioned asked themselves how not to succumb to temptation, how not to decode every page like a *roman à clef* (but Proust never carried the set of keys out of his apartment). The question was whether someday it would be possible to read him as one could read La Bruyère or Balzac, without swooning at resemblances, without trying to recognize Charles Haas or Boni de Castellane, without seeing Madame Straus, Misia Sert, the Countess Greffulhe, Louis d'Albufera or Laure Hayman filtering through the onionskin.

An old school friend, Robert Dreyfus, makes a wish. He imagines this is how posterity will read Proust, in a century or two, 'if, of course, it enjoys any intellectual pleasures beyond watching movies or listening to the radio, and if our great-great-nephews still know how to read – I mean really read – which is not at all certain.' So he writes in an article in the *Journal des débats* that he republishes, word for word, in 1939… As if it were business as usual, as if there were no gaping abyss, as if the existence of great-great-nephews was the least improbable thing in the world to come.

Also in the year 1939, one Sunday afternoon, March 5th, in her bookshop on the Rue de l'Odéon, La Maison des Amis des Livres, Adrienne Monnier opens a permanent exhibition of writers' portraits by Gisèle Freund, in the medium of color photography. To be sure, Marcel Proust is not represented, but all the others are there: tousle-haired Cocteau, Gide 'with his pure and mortified features', Paul Valéry, Claudel, André Breton, Jules Romains, Romain Rolland, Léon-Paul Fargue, Colette, and Sartre, and Simone de Beauvoir, Aragon, and Joyce, and Virginia Woolf, and Walter Benjamin (who had been perhaps the first to spot 'the satanic enchantment' in Proustian reportage), all of them at once embalmed or jellified in the timed pose, wrinkled and blotched more than usual, yet revitalized by the Kodachrome emulsion.

Still Alive

Why do biographies never begin with words other than the customary? Why not these, for instance: 'Deceased in Paris on the 18th of November, 1922, Marcel Proust now resides in the 20th arrondissement, not far from the Place Gambetta…'

Jacques-Émile Blanche recounts how on the fifth anniversary of Proust's death, his friends, who met regularly, fantasized that he was still alive. He had become a member of the Goncourt Academy, a doctor *honoris causa* at an incredible number of European and American universities, his time entirely taken up with speeches, juries, prizes, banquets, review articles, prefaces, manuscripts to read, interviews, international appearances.

What if he had outlived himself? Instead of disappearing at the very moment of fruition, would he have had time to polish *Le Temps retrouvé;* to read over and correct the complete edition of his book, riddled as it was with approximations and incalculable mistakes; to revise *Du côté de chez Swann*, which he reproached himself for having published prematurely, before it was possible to see the whole picture; and even, who knows, to rewrite the entire manuscript, which would have become the starting point for still another *Recherche*?

Would Cocteau have introduced him to the Côte

d'Azur, persuaded him to play himself in *The Blood of a Poet*, appearing in a box with the Viscount and Viscountess de Noailles, the Prince and Princess de Faucigny-Lucinges, and Lady Abdy (all of whom subsequently demanded they be cut from the film)?

Would Paul Morand have persuaded him to accompany him to New York? Would he have been present at the premiere of Charlie Chaplin's *City Lights*, then gone on to explore Istanbul, Berlin, Moscow, Kyoto? In response to the rightwing anti-Parliamentarist demonstrations of 1934, would he finally have broken with Léon Daudet? Thanks to René Blum, who recommended him to the publisher Bernard Grasset, would he have reconnected with one of his schoolmates at the Lycée Condorcet, Léon Blum?

Still sick, would he have become a recluse once and for all, moving again and again, so that all traces of him would be lost? Would he have walled himself up and withdrawn from the world, so that the strangest rumors spread about him periodically, transforming his secret bedroom into the dark heart of Paris? Would he have taken a vow of silence, so that his absence would be felt as a reproach to all those who continued to appear on the public stage?

Would he once again have been a witness to disaster, to nameless horror in the very land of culture and civilization? Would the experts have discoursed learnedly, serenely, on the question of whether the law that Vichy could not wait to promulgate (Vichy, where his doctors and his brother might, between the two world wars, have recommended that he go to take the waters) – whether the first law and then the second on the status of Jews applied to him? Consulted, jurists would not have failed to conclude that the gentleman Proust Marcel did not meet all the necessary criteria. Unlike his mother, born Jeanne Weil, if she had still been of this world, or his 'dear cousin' by marriage, Henri Bergson (who was especially grateful to the writer for recommending the use of earplugs): when the time came, in the autumn of 1940, the philosopher insisted on registering at police headquarters in Passy.

Proust's destiny could have been the twin of Paul Valéry's, born the same year as he, but deceased in 1945. He might have passed away – why not? – in 1951, like André Gide (his senior by two years), or in 1954, like Colette (two years his junior), in 1955, like Paul Claudel (who was three years older), or even in the early Sixties ... Hadn't his great friend Reynaldo Hahn outlived him by thirty years?

Paris-Prague

On November 14th, 1922, as Proust expends what little strength he still has on revising his book, Franz Kafka, who for the past month and a half had not written one line in his journal, takes up his pen. He notes that he always has a fever in the evening, that he cannot get anything done at his worktable, he scarcely goes out, he no longer visits the streets of Prague. 'Despite this, I would be behaving like Tartuffe if I complained of being sick.'

Kafka is not yet forty. He has eighteen months to live, eighteen months more than Proust.

Imaginary Lives

To justify the surprising principle which underlies his *Imaginary Lives*, whose publication − like that of Remy de Gourmont's *Book of Masks*, illustrated by Félix Vallotton − dates from 1896, the year of the invention of the cinematograph, Marcel Schwob asserted that if the ideas of great men arise from 'humanity's common patrimony', then there is nothing distinctive about any one of these individuals except his eccentricities. A subject on which biographies generally remain silent. In his opinion, the lives of the illustrious should on the contrary be painted in terms of their anomalies, like those Japanese prints that reproduce, over and over, the image of a caterpillar seen only once at one specific hour of the day.

Thus, in the ghost story that is *Nadja*, André Breton evokes the little private ceremony that Victor Hugo repeated daily at the end of his life. Travelling the same route for the thousandth time with Juliette Drouet, he broke their silence only as the carriage passed an estate framed by two gates, one large and one small. 'The rider's gate, madame', he said to Juliette, indicating the large entryway. 'Sir, the pedestrian gate', she replied, passing before the little one, while Hugo, a little farther along, in front of two interlaced trees, invariably pronounced the phrase: 'Philemon and Baucis.'

Breton read this anecdote as the best possible commentary on Hugo's work. 'How pleased I would be to possess data as valuable as this about each of the men I admire,' he concluded.

As for Victor Hugo, he made note in his *Things Seen* of the last visit he paid Balzac, the other giant of the century, a few hours before the end. Apart from the doctor, Hugo was the only one to come to his bedside that day, to brave the ordeal. 'The real truth is that Balzac died abandoned by everyone and everything, like a dog', Octave Mirbeau elaborated.

Mirbeau based his statement, in 1905, on confidences he'd supposedly received, as had Rodin, from an old painter named Jean Gigoux, who described Balzac's household as even more forsaken than Hugo supposed, and who admitted that he, Gigoux, had denied himself even a pencil sketch of the deceased. Why, given that he was present in a nearby room? Because he'd just made love there with Balzac's wife, the ex-Madame Hanska.

Her daughter objected vehemently to this story, on the grounds that her mother did not even meet the painter until two years after that infamous night. True or false, Mirbeau had to blue-pencil the episode, although it illustrated marvelously, if at the expense of the superhuman author of *The Human Comedy*, his theory of biography. No, he wrote, a great man need not necessarily be a sympathetic, virtuous, heroic individual – along the lines of poor Verlaine, whom some had turned into a sort of decent bourgeois. To enter into posterity, we must call an end to extreme unction: 'It is through his sins that a great man fascinates us the most. It is through Rousseau's weaknesses, his inanities, his indignities, his crimes, and all the painful struggles these presuppose, that he moves us to tears, and that we venerate him, cherish him.'

Proust died at the age of fifty-one, the same age as Balzac.

The Visible Body

What is the *life of an author*?

The visible body encloses the other, invisible, subterranean. The real body, simultaneously hidden and revealed by the first, the 'worldly' body. The one that was gifted with speech, the one that was photographed, the one with which others crossed paths. Quirks, manias, obsessions, moods, wounds, weaknesses, rage, all that which has nothing to do with the little heap of meetings and dates that reassure collectors.

History leaves the individual life unclear. Only art can locate it, thought Hofmannsthal, who added: 'The portraitist is related to the biographer and the biographer to the actor.'

The cracked tiles beneath our feet in the miniscule passage that never ends, the wall still splashed with the projection from the magic lantern, the imprint of a neck on a feather bolster, the first floor of the summer home on the Rue du Saint-Esprit, the childhood bed, still made up, untouched, like the interior of a little tomb... What the writer's eyes saw, what his senses perceived, it is these that mesmerize and lure us in pursuit of him, until we finally wonder just how far we can go in our turn, which footsteps we can walk in.

Deep-Sea Diver*

The waiting and the cold will have to be endured. In an abandoned warehouse, crammed with old clothes, I try on gloves, hats, top hats. I put on trousers, shirts, tailcoats, dickeys, frock coats, overcoats.

One of the rare times in his life when he saw Proust, recounted Léon-Paul Fargue, they had gone to hear Ricardo Viñes play Ravel or Debussy. Facing the piano, the two men drowsed shoulder to shoulder, perfectly immobile, impeccably constricted in their ceremonial uniforms, encased. How many hours a day were required to get dressed and undressed? The essential thing in the life of a man about town was not to wrinkle. Neither folds nor puckers, no crumpling, above all *hold onto yourself,* that is, remain rigid.

It is still dark when they dress me, comb me, curl me, hairpiece me, powder me. The moustaches instantly age me by a century. The ghost on Boulevard Haussmann has cast a spell on me for violating his deserted house.

The castle at Champlâtreux might still belong to the de Noailles family. Immense galleries like Sleeping Beauty's residence brought back to life. Drawing rooms,

---

*Jérôme Prieur played Monsieur Verdurin in Raúl Ruiz's internationally acclaimed feature film *Time Regained* (1999). The author's diary of the filming, *Chez Proust en tournant,* was published in 2016.

bedchambers, vestibules, billiard rooms, here and there another world establishes itself, and we tumble into it, all the while avoiding the watchmens' rounds. Men in black opera hats plucked from Magritte's paintings, women plumed in egret, straight out of *Fantomas*... Waking up early, lunching early, without understanding why, the back and forth from one meal to the next, even the huge aprons, white as camisoles, in which we are enveloped in the canteen, our slightest activity always under escort, up and down the staircases and corridors, all this intensifies our sense, as we go on, of having been committed to a sanatorium, where finally we are delivered to our destination, the operating theatre.

You get used to everything, the powder that erases the bags under your eyes, the poisonous smell of glue and the tickling of the brush beneath the nostrils as the moustache gets attached, since I have to appear twenty years younger than yesterday. At the Verdurins', the narrator, who does not take part in the frivolous conversation, is conspicuously elsewhere, ignored by everyone, almost never speaking, absent but always present, missing nothing. The child Marcel crosses a vast drawing room populated with ancestors in evening dress who whisper to each other, exhausted from talking. He progresses, followed by his shadow, the narrator, then by his adult double, with a maharajah's profile.

Fragments of faces behind their portholes, bodies enveloped by explorers' costumes and accoutrements. Undressed, dressed up, undercover, in cosmetics, incognito, I climb into a diving suit that will permit me to descend 20,000 leagues beneath the sea, into the vast depths of *À la recherche du temps perdu.*

In his theatre box, little Marcel paces up and down.

Dead City

In the evenings, from the church of the Madeleine to Saint-Antoine, the whole district is dark, all the lights are out, no living creature remains behind the extinguished windows. The cork bedroom in the apartment on Boulevard Haussmann serves now as a temporary office.

The little Rue Hamelin, where Proust came to finish his life, remains almost the same as it was during his era, renovated but still bleak, white as a bone washed clean by intemperate weather. Does it owe its name and its mysterious pull to the legend of the pied piper of Hamelin, the musician who succeeded in luring all the children out of the city he had saved from plague-bearing rats?

The roadway is no longer cobblestoned. The wine merchant, the art supply shop and the greengrocer, the dairy and the ironmonger, the bookshop whose window had so dazzled Céleste when she perceived that the pages of the books on display looked like angels' wings – all commerce has disappeared, except for an Arab grocery store on the ground floor of the house, now open day and night.

Pointless to cross the threshold, pointless to ask to go upstairs, nothing is the same: the building has been a commercial hotel for some time now. The interior has been demolished: you would look in vain for even the lift cage, the mahogany banister, the worn stairs, the carpet that cushioned the steps of visitors, the metal latticework on the lift door, the little stained-glass windows that might have been found at every landing, or the bulbs in their opaline glass corollas…

Even the church of Saint-Pierre de Chaillot, a few hundred meters away, where the funeral was held on an autumn morning, can no longer serve as witness to anything. The building was razed at the end of the Thirties. Another construction has replaced it, in the affluent modernist style so dear to pre-war architecture.

Everything is still there, everything is in ruins.

You can almost see the eviscerated interior walls, the stove-in ceilings, the torn-up floors, and where the bedroom once was, behind the bed, the original widestriped wallpaper, now coming unglued. The whole house, with its branching nerves, its muscle fibers, its abdominal cavity and braincase, resembles a flayed anatomical model.

In the Shop Window

Living rooms, dining rooms, bedrooms, all giving directly onto the pavement: in the past, the Faubourg Saint-Antoine offered a theatrical display of furniture boutiques. The street was nothing but a wall of images, while in its sample apartments and model homes, vast sofas languished behind plate-glass windows and despair hovered when prospective tenants were slow to breach the threshold.

In the labyrinth of the Carnavalet Museum, a guard finally agrees to unlock the gallery which is always closed when you want to see it: the Gallery of Writers' Bedrooms. A single glance takes it all in, you hardly need to step back, in the same space is the boudoir of the young Anna de Noailles, the catch-all clutter of Paul Léautaud, the bedchamber of Marcel Proust.

At the heart of the dormitory, harshly lit by neon, Marcel's bedroom, his strongroom, reinforced like a submarine, is too narrow. Tiny copper bed, appearing freshly polished beneath its petroleum-blue stole. Mountain of too-rare curios in the meagre space, flimsy nightstand on which a bottle of black ink lies abandoned between two or three school notebooks, still blank. These souvenirs do not feel real, this is the stage set for a stylish boulevard vaudeville.

Returning

The long black cloak has been tossed across the blue bed.

As if the electrician who came to change the lurid neon light that scours the room and scorches the eyes had forgotten to pick up his jacket. Or could a visitor have taken advantage of the guards' momentary distraction by leaving his 'visiting card', as was the custom in the past among society ladies?

This old piece of clothing, supposedly Proust's, made its appearance one day in the facsimile of his bedroom at the Carnavalet. But it's no more than a corpse. Its forlorn black plumage clashes too much with the almost sterile neatness of the place, where even the bedspread seems to have just returned from the dry cleaner's.

The bed with its copper bed knobs, the nightstand, the portrait on the wall, the empty display case are sacred objects. But you might more easily believe yourself in a salesroom or the Grévin Wax Museum than inside one of the inviolate tombs of ancient Egypt.

Today, at 102 Boulevard Haussmann, the original bedroom where almost all of *La Recherche* was written is closed to admirers. No more pilgrims are admitted there to contemplate the void. It seems the bank that owns the building has big plans.

'Monsieur Proust is dead!'

Voices from beyond the grave, tinny voices pass the word by telephone: 'Monsieur is dead!' 'Marcel just died!' He who over the years had so often found himself at death's door, he who chronically could not go on, who claimed so many times that he was dying, then apologized for it with such winning grace, this time it was true.

The streets of Paris are even emptier on Sunday.

The city is deserted, as in dreams. It resembles night, those strange nights when it is broad daylight outside.

Céleste opens the door, she is a ghost, she is ashen.

The address, kept secret, is 44 Rue Hamelin.

Driven out by the bank that had bought his aunt's building, where he was cocooned, driven out by the fear of construction and his panic at noise, he had resigned himself to emigrating to a provincial street, safely tucked away behind the Étoile (the unknown soldier had just been honored, one week earlier, beneath the Arc de Triomphe).

It was a twin sister to tiny Rue Laurent-Pichat, where, after the Boulevard Haussmann, he had been housed for three months – the last holiday, the last trip to the edge of the Bois de Boulogne, whose curtain of trees he had been unable to admire until after the wartime curfew.

The Mummy

The blinds are closed, the double curtains drawn.

Neither daylight nor fresh air must get into the bedroom, for fear they might injure the man asleep there. You could already mistake him for a mummy.

Cocteau recounts: 'On his childhood bed Proust offered the admirable profile of a vizier. He wore the beard he used to grow then shave off, then grow out, and which, after a long absence, you were never sure you'd see again. This beard, which when he was alive seemed almost a joke, as fake as that of the dead Sadi Carnot at the Grévin Wax Museum, this beard hiding the curved jaw of Jacques-Émile Blanche's young dandy, behind which he used to titter as though behind a woman's fan, this beard on his cadaver became the attribute of a magus and a king.'

Likeness

Under the pretext of viewing the body, it is the enigma of the character we wish to catch sight of. Impossible *Open, Sesame!* The transaction partakes of magic, of sorcery.

The secret is that of likeness. But likeness in the paradoxical sense defined by Jean Paulhan, in one of the texts he devotes to Cubist painting, an artistic revolution that occurred, incidentally, at exactly the same period when *La Recherche* was taking shape. Thus Paulhan stated that he did not believe in ghosts, all the while acknowledging that he was wrong. He added, 'It is a bad day for us when we are shown our profile in the play of mirrors, or hear our own voice in a recording, or read our old love letters, and in that moment we have an urge to scream. It is so obvious to us that we are anything but *that*. Accurate photos, faithful portraits can be powerful, subtle, beautiful or ugly. They have one trait in common of far greater importance: they don't resemble us.' In fact, resemblance is always, accurate or inaccurate, a surprise. Innocent X was simultaneously painted by Velásquez and sculpted by Bernini. But the sovereign pontiff did not care for the overly pink flesh portrayed by the former, nor, in the work of the latter, his white marble nose or chin. He looked 'too real'; it horrified him.

Except for his beard, Lev Nikolayevich Tolstoy has a family likeness to Innocent X which should have interested physiognomists. On September 3rd, 1909, the novelist writes in his journal, 'Two cinematographers arrived, despite my refusal. I let them go ahead, but without participating myself.' Two weeks later, he narrates the end of his adventure: 'Woke up alert. A photographer and a cinematographer presented themselves. Doubly disagreeable because it induces a consciousness of self not as divine but as the abominable L. N.'

Baudelaire kept one single photograph from among all those that Félix Nadar took of him. A blurred shot, a shaky image. This anticipated Paulhan's view: namely, that we cannot see and recognize ourselves in any known physical form, not as portraits represent us, nor as cutaways, nor, of course, as skeletons. But only as ghosts.

His Mark

One year after his death, 'at the end of the year of Proust', in the time-honored expression of the era, one of his confidants bemoans the fact that *everyone* wants to have been among his friends.

The Slavic princesses and rich Bostonian ladies who had besieged him ('I, too – I am a writer!' they were quick to claim, as one equal to another), all these will descend on Paris to write dissertations, definitive works. Having failed to gain access to the great man, they must at the very least meet those who knew him, those who saw him with their own eyes.

One day a young woman falls from the sky, or rather from Colorado, to land on the doorstep of one such. No, don't bother discussing the work, evoking the author, describing the man, the American immediately stops him. He needn't even bother to open his mouth.

'I just wanted to know what an old friend of Proust's was made of.' What does he look like, the man who saw the man who saw the bear.

Sacha Guitry

Proust was buried on November 22nd, 1922. Strange coincidence: seven years earlier, to the day, November 22nd, 1915, Sacha Guitry's film *Those of Our Land* opened at the Théâtre des Variétés.

'I do not want your grandchildren,' explained the promoter, 'to come to me fifty years from now and say: "What, my good old man, you were alive at the same time as Claude Monet... and you didn't think to film him at work?" Well, your grandchildren will not say any such thing to me because I did, I did think of it... I've often said to myself: what a thrill it would be if suddenly we were shown Praxiteles sculpting this marble, Rembrandt finishing that self-portrait, Shakespeare writing the dedication on the original script of *Hamlet*, Mozart at the harpsichord, Voltaire coining witticisms. Think what a Maillol statue would be, were it sculpted before a camera, which recorded it from the hour of its birth to the hour of its completion.'

The shooting of the film dates back to late 1914, at the beginning of the Great War. Today almost ridiculous, the title blatantly emphasizes that the film was meant to be understood as an act of patriotism, in reaction to the 'Manifesto of the Ninety-Three,' a proclamation of support for German military actions signed by ninety-three prominent German intellectuals in 1914. The film was a monument erected to the French mind – a gesture of the kind that Proust always energetically rejected, loathing the chauvinism that led more than one individual to boycott Goethe or Wagner, cordially despising all flag-wavers (among them, Camille Saint-Saëns).

Complimenting his secretary and valet, a big Swede named Ernst Forssgren who had launched into 'La Marseillaise' for the soldiers convalescing at the Cabourg infirmary, Proust hastened to assure him he was 'altogether like Sacha Guitry.' It was the young man himself, bursting with pride, who reported this, missing Proust's malice (and perhaps confusing Guitry father and son).

As for the budding dramatic author, of course he did not want to be accused of draft-dodging, but he was sufficiently wealthy not to need to resort to trickery. Rather, we must suppose he had an altogether different motive for making the film: that of resisting, with anything that came to hand, the hecatomb which was unfolding. Of saving from the looming annihilation a few figures, a few major figures. The mad desire to give to these immortals, in the midst of this preamble to mass butchery, eternal life. As Remy de Gourmont wrote in the September 1907 issue of *Mercure de France:* 'Film actors perform only once, and it lasts for years; their gestures captured, they might all perish in a catastrophe, but the performance would continue nonetheless, always identical to itself.'

The Birdman

In the early 1900s, inside a darkened room or beneath a fairground tent, could Proust have seen the images of a news item, a performance recorded live? A little documentary, shot by a cameraman for Gaumont: the man who wanted to fly, filmed by a camera on the first level of the Eiffel Tower, just before his departure.

Contrary to one's memory of it, the shot lasts a long time, forty or so seconds. The individual, apparently a tailor, harnessed into a special outfit of his own making, which causes him to resemble a bird without wings, clambers boldly over the guardrail.

He spends the last instants of his existence before the eyes of his public, and our own. We would like to warn him, to escape the nightmare into which he is leading us, to stop watching. There he is, perched over the void, the void the camera never shows but that we dread, the void we perceive in the little hesitancies of the birdman, in his jerks, his jolts, his impulses forward, instantly checked, which seem to last an eternity – until at last he makes his mind up, disappearing off camera, undoubtedly plummeting like a stone with all his weight, instead of floating on the air.

Those of Our Land

Rodin paces back and forth like a wild beast in his studio in the Hôtel Biron. He turns to Sacha Guitry's camera, looks into the lens, freezes for an instant as if posing in the photographer's studio, then goes back to tapping his chisel. 'Tell me to stop when you begin, so I don't move,' he may have said to the amateur film-maker. Camille Saint-Saëns is playing the piano, for once facing the audience. He raises a masterful hand to conduct an orchestra all the more silent for being imaginary. The lawyer Henri Robert flings himself into a blazing oral argument even though the court session is perfectly fictional. Anatole France arranges piles of books in his new library. Antoine, the theatre director, rehearses two actors in *The School for Wives*. Renoir, his fingers paralyzed, never stops painting, aided by his son Jean who squeezes out the paints for him. On his property in Giverny, Monet is at work. He seems an emanation of the aquatic flora and the film's silver nitrate.

The master of ceremonies floods these mute images with his own verbiage, as if he must at all cost fill the void. He saturates the film to such a degree that we are made to see the invisible with our own eyes. Even death at work, the death that dances around the living: that of Octave Mirbeau, exhausted by life; that of Monet, as Clemenceau (recounts Sacha Guitry) rushes in his carriage to the painter's bedside, to embrace his old friend one last time.

We do not hear, we can no longer hear, what these extraordinary characters are saying. During the Fifties, in the first years of television, when Guitry completed his film, he did not attempt to reconstruct their phrases, as might a deaf-mute, by reading their lips.

Acting like an anesthetic, Sacha Guitry's voice prevents us above all from noticing that everyone, or almost everyone, is possessed by a veritable craving for talk. They never stop talking to someone who is at times present, at times absent from the shot, but whose company is never in doubt: a friend.

Which is to say that the portraitist of *Those of Our Land* is not filming Great Men, who might have wished to address posterity through him. He is filming close friends, regulars, confidants, who are addressing him and him alone.

Thus in this film, the first of its kind, some act for the camera, others pursue their work. Some put on a performance of their role, others perform it for real, but nobody is making believe. The painters paint – and it is they who are the most indifferent to how they look. Dressed all in white and filled with high spirits, Sarah Bernhardt is handed a page on which a poem has been copied out. She reads it tenderly to the young Sacha, who is seated on the bench beside her, a straw boater on his head. She bursts out laughing, she could almost be mistaken for Colette – the young Proust, too, danced attendance on her. Octave Mirbeau does not write as he is being filmed; later, Edmond Rostand resigns himself to the task. Anatole France follows his example. Seated at a table, he resolves to write a message to his interlocutor, despite the faulty pen loaned him by the housemaid. Signing his autograph, he doesn't execute the flourish we expect, the enormous smudge that some remember. His pen does catch on the paper and deposits two inkblots along the way, but we can only intuit them, not see them. Anatole France blots them on his trousers, the voiceover assures us, unfazed by such a trifle.

The age and the uniqueness of the footage in *Those of Our Land* is obviously what makes it priceless, but the unease we gradually begin to feel arises from elsewhere. We scan the shot of a bustling Parisian street: almost immediately, searching for a familiar face among the pedestrians on the Boulevard de Clichy, we recognize Edgar Degas. Escorted by a female companion, Degas – who, the voiceover explains, did not wish to be filmed – walks toward us. He advances in our direction, without avoiding us but paying us no attention, not even noticing us. He does not turn his back, as we would swear he's going to. He is unaware of us, all the more so since he has almost entirely lost his eyesight.

Degas is the only one to be ambushed against his will. And yet, aren't they all like him: blind, since they do not see us?

A revealing detail: of all those being filmed, only Sacha Guitry glances repeatedly at the camera. Is he worried about what the cameraman is doing or not doing, is he making sure the camera is rolling? Certainly, but he is breaching, without knowing it, without wanting to, the impassable barrier between the screen (where he exists) and the auditorium (where we exist), between two different worlds. He is trying to shuttle back and forth between the living and the dead.

There is more. This silent and too-fleeting film astonishes the viewer and proves unforgettable even to those who have only seen it once simply because it is such a stunning demonstration of the art of portrait.

The portrait, that is, the relationship between the painter and his model, is not a window, but a theater in miniature. Or more precisely, a trap – even if you are not exactly sure of what you're going to catch, or even what you're hunting. A trap where adoration and devotion belong as much as cruelty.

Cabourg, 1914

Marcel Proust was not filmed by Sacha Guitry.

In fact, Marcel Proust was never filmed at all.

What would the film have looked like if Proust had appeared in it, if these two men had not cordially ignored one another?

Whom would the author of *Du côté de chez Swann* have looked like?

Sherlock Holmes?

The sky and the sandy beach in front of the Grand Hotel are very overexposed, since it is necessary to shoot in full daylight.

A silhouette is advancing along the seawall. The man is always armed with an umbrella, to protect himself against the last rays of the sun. He never takes off his heavy pearl-grey woolen overcoat, which dates from the distant past. We cannot see that its lining is mauve satin.

In late September, toward the end of the afternoon, the light is so tender, and the air breathable. It is 1914, the last summer of the century. Proust has come to Cabourg for the last time in his life.

His Voice

Proust was mad about the telephone, and it was thanks to the passable approximation of the Théâtrophone that in February 1911, he could enjoy, in his own home, Act III of *Die Meistersinger*, then several days later *Pélléas et Mélisande*, transmitted directly from the Opéra-Comique. But his voice is unknown to us.

Inevitably, we imagine it as Apollinaire's voice wearily droning, under torrential rain, 'Le Pont Mirabeau,' etched into a wax disk as black as a slice of anthracite.

Proust's friends will describe how when reading his work they instinctively copy his diction, his slightly sing-song tone, the distant quality of his voice like that of a storyteller in the Far East. When he speaks, he paces a labyrinth of interminable sentences, unwinding it before him as he goes. His immense monologues are all meanderings, digressions, reservations, regrets, which those present wish they could memorize. The flow is modulated, says Jean Cocteau, by a cunning system of constraints and sluice gates, of slight pauses governed by his syntax, of different keyboards on which he tinkles away.

His voice is sweet, almost honeyed, some add. Muffled, you might say, cautious, monotone perhaps, or rather faltering; the sounds seem to be formed beyond the teeth and lips, somewhere other than the throat. It is the voice of a ventriloquist.

Waves from the Past

'I wished to fix the tones, the grace,
Reflected in the mirror's face
– The pleasures of an opera ball,
Jade shadows, ruby hours late –
Forever on the inert plate.
Such was my wish; it shall befall.
I wished for voices I have loved,
Like features in a gem engraved,
To last forever and a day
And sing with undiminished power
The dreams of every too-brief hour.
Time wants to flee; I make it stay.'

The author of these verses from *The Necklace of Claws*, Charles Cros, was also the inventor of the phonograph. From the very beginning, the recording of sounds was felt, like photography, to be a violent extraction of pieces of the past, the present never being more than imminent past, potential past.

Carlo Dossi, a diplomat mad for erudition and enamored of archeology (who ended his career as plenipotentiary of the kingdom of Italy in Athens at the end of the 19th century), scrawled an even more dizzying proposition in his *Note azzure*, the personal notebooks that would be published after his death.

There he imagines that music will someday be put in tins, 'like tuna or sardines.' Then, just by piercing a hole, the sound waves will begin to vibrate and we will hear a sonata, a whole opera, a dog-and-cat fight, or an ancestor's last will and testament.

The idea that nothing in the universe is ever truly lost may simply — or perhaps not so simply — originate from particle physics. Press your ear to the wall, blow off the accumulated dust, scratch away the sands of time: antiquity is right here, as if it all happened yesterday, suspended layer by layer in the ether.

'Let us remove a shard from an ancient Roman house,' writes Dossi. 'We will extract, by means of the Phonoextractor, the sounds adhering to it and store them in receptacles. The first sounds will of course be the most recently recorded, and the words will enter the receptacle backwards. But once the receptacle is reversed, they will right themselves. And then — to the immense joy of Latinists — we will be present for the conversations of Roman emperors and slaves, we will hear Etruscan religious chants, debates in the Senate, the diverse roarings of barbarians...'

Several months after Sacha Guitry's film, in 1916, Guillaume Apollinaire will go so far as to imagine, in *The Moon King*, that pleasures and inadmissible desires might be stored and served up to audiences as dizzying chasms of sensation for the body and soul. Proust's friend and mentor Léon Daudet, an author of science fiction in his spare time, will in turn fabricate a machine, under the brand name Dyonisos, that captures waves of the past. By means of a certain space-time conjunction, the apparatus has the remarkable power to suck spectators into the interior of the projected images, the interior of the time-hallucination, as if their gaze were dragging the whole body after it into the void, into the field of a kind of gigantic stereoscopic vision, increasing perception tenfold, calling forth transgressions beyond those of the laws of physics.

Scents

Proust had long been fascinated by this kind of magical object. In February 1901, he submits to the *Chronicle of Arts and Curiosities* his review of a slim booklet published by Robert de Montesquiou, entitled *Land of Scents*. The pages on which Proust comments served as a guide to one of the most minuscule spectacles offered to visitors to the 1900 World's Fair pavilions: the Victor Klotz collection in the Retrospective of Perfumery.

Montesquiou, Proust's 'Professor of Beauty,' had indulged himself in systematically imagining what could not possibly be exhibited at the 1900 World's Fair, yet leapt to the mind's eye: Esther's hair, steeped for six months in oil of myrrh before her introduction to Ahasuerus; the strawberry and raspberry baths in which the 'marvelous' Madame Tallien, Our Lady of Thermidor, softened her skin; the horror of roses experienced by Marie de Medici, who fainted at mere sight of them; the musk that Empress Joséphine was mad for; even the heat of climbing vines and the cool of forests; neroli and frangipani; the purple odor of a corpse poisoned by cyanide…

The young Proust's throat and lungs did not tolerate the slightest hint of the faintest perfume – but his favorite, it is said, was 'Habanita' by Molinard. What captivated his sense of smell inflicted torments on him.

Which is to say that when he ambles, if only in the imagination, through the literary museum of perfumery that Montesquiou offers him, Proust is playing with fire. His review is very careful not to cite even one stanza of the litany of malevolent names: this would be to give form to an incantation that he cannot commit to paper, but which he must have whispered while reading and rereading the guide to perfumes.

The young Proust banishes from his writing any fragrance that might tickle his nostrils. He does not give any name to scents, does not name one of the saps or spices vaporized by Montesquiou, does not pick even one flower, with the sole exception of hydrangeas, though their petals are a little withered – this, a gallant nod to the author of *Blue Hydrangeas*.

For once, Proust remains abstract, to such a degree that it must be deliberate. He scarcely touches on the anthology of citations, but emphasizes the nomenclature that completes it. It is containers that fascinate him, containers that he can talk about in place of the contained: cases, compacts, vials, little boxes, vases, flasks.

He has no need to open incense-burners or 'boxes of scent' in order to release that which he will spend his life in search of: 'something so troubling and so delicious, although the least material of things, the melancholy odor, the imperishable Perfume of the Past.'

Cinematograph

Why, then, does Proust detest the Cinematograph as much as he claims to?

When he consents to mention it, once, he does so with distaste, in the guise of a metaphor. He explains *a contrario* that the modern novel cannot possibly be the brief concise overview that certain young people have demanded. If it were this, then 'a sort of cinematographic procession, a defile' would suffice, he grimaces (and also undoubtedly lets fly a personal barb at his dear cousin by marriage – Bergson, who in *Creative Evolution* built his philosophy of consciousness on this very metaphor).

Defile, defilement, the expression must be heard in all its ambiguity. In his eyes (but no one knows if he is basing this on mere hearsay) film is at best a feat of railway engineering or a martial art. A craft that establishes a cadence and cuts the world into pieces, organized, infinitely regulated, uniform. Troop movements or the crossing of a landscape by train: what is given us to see is the machine's point of view, a mechanical perspective. From which, by definition, is excluded the accidental, the unforeseen.

Seeing Proust manipulate, in service to his cause, this little train and these little soldiers, old childhood toys that lack the virtues of his magic lantern, we cannot help but sense his blindness. Not to say his bad faith, in contrast to his exhilaration at the ubiquity conveyed by the automobile and the airplane.

Proust does not dismiss the cinema as a mere subsidiary of the theater, though most of his enlightened contemporaries do — not to mention those artists, members of the blossoming French avant-garde, who devoted themselves to the search for 'pure cinema.'

Rather, he pretends to believe that the strip of film would inevitably communicate to images its own perpetual movement, its uninterrupted course: supposedly, it would preclude changing direction, light, or speed; slowing or accelerating; pulling back for a long-distance shot; moving in gradually close enough to dilate the infinitesimal particle; working the materiality of time. Isn't film incapable, he asks, of giving us 'the taste of the morning *café au lait*' that we used to drink from a white porcelain bowl 'which seemed itself to be milk crystallized, when the day was still intact and full?'

If in saying the same words, we all perceived the same things, if we all thought alike, if everyone knew what we meant when we said, 'Bad weather, a war, a cab stand, a lighted restaurant, a garden in bloom,' then reality would be more or less identical for all of us. And 'if reality were this sort of waste product of past experience,' Proust continues in *Le Temps retrouvé*, 'if reality were that, doubtless a sort of cinematographic film of these things would be enough.'

The unbreachable chasm was clear (and from 1911 to 1922, the manuscripts do not show a single word changed in this categorical sentence).

But shouldn't the very argument used to impugn the cinema be turned inside out like a glove? Wouldn't a mere nothing have been enough to throw everything off balance, so that 'so-called "lived" art, as simple as life itself, bereft of beauty, a boring and pointless duplicate of what our eyes see and our intelligence observes,' would in fact make us recognize 'the very reality from which we live at such a distance'?

A mere nothing for the miraculous palpitations of involuntary memory to pulverize all clichés and uncover the treasure beneath the rubble — since experience is never mutual, but by its very nature intensely unique. A mere nothing to recapture — in the artificial night, at the heart of the projection of luminous particles — the improbable astonishment that takes hold of us before the emptiest of things, the taste that certain days awaken in us, at the end of the afternoon, 'that reality which we risk dying without ever having known, and which is, quite simply, our life.'

The End of the World

In the summer of 1922, an American scholar once again announces that the end of the world is imminent. A reporter for the daily newspaper *L'Intransigeant* asks several celebrities of the moment what they would do if this time it were true.

'I think life would suddenly seem delicious to us,' answers Marcel Proust. 'Just imagine how many projects, travel plans, passions, areas of study it – our life – holds in suspension, invisible to us in our laziness, which, assured of a future, continually postpones them. But should all that threaten to become impossible forever, how beautiful it would become again... And yet we shouldn't require a cataclysm to love life today. It would have been enough to reflect that we are human and death may come tonight.'

Proust's funeral took place on the 22nd of the following November. It was a Wednesday.

'What a beautiful service! But I always thought our young man was Jewish...' whispers the delicate Maurice Barrès, planted on the sidewalk of the Avenue Marceau, in front of Saint-Pierre de Chaillot – where Proust had never before set foot. The organist played Ravel, whose music Proust did not really care for: *Pavane for a Dead Princess*... For what obscure reason? Nobody could have said who had played this trick on him, taunting him, mocking him.

The walls of the church are hung in black. Too many hangings, too many candles, too much music, murmur the companions of his youth.

Dukes and duchesses send coded messages to each other, princes and countesses congregate, there are members of The Jockey Club, and – why not? – the Russian Ballet, a detachment of the constitutional body, the House, the Senate, the Academy he dreamed of, the regulars as usual in mourning, and several young avant-garde poets... To the list of unfortunates who not even for an empire would have missed the ultimate reception, a Parisian chronicler does not hesitate to add 'the great Parisian pederasty, past their prime,' faces powdered, nails painted, glances prying.

But few men of letters, the gossiping tongues deplore. Less than four hundred, minimize the jealous (who, like most, could not for a moment have imagined what the future held).

'A thousand friends,' corrects one of the latter, 'who know what they have lost.'

November 1922

That week, between the 16th and the 22nd of November, *Nosferatu the Vampyre* opened in Paris (without much success), at the Ciné-Opéra.

Also in November 1922, Vladimir Mayakovsky is staying in the capital. The Bolshevik poet is on a field trip. He inspects, observes, is astonished. He asks to meet a great writer, suggesting two names: Anatole France, Henri Barbusse. His guide smiles at such bad taste: rather, he must meet 'the French Dostoevsky,' Marcel Proust.

No use: it is November 17th, and Proust is *in extremis*. The Russian writer can only be present at his funeral, surrounded by what he believes to be the pride of artistic and official Paris.

Funeral Procession

The weather is dry, the sky clear and almost cloudless.

A carriage overflowing with flowers precedes the funeral procession, which will traverse the whole Rive Droite on foot, along the boulevards. Toward noon they begin to descend the Champs-Elysées. Then Avenue Gabriel and the Marigny Theater, which housed the panorama of bygone battles, where in the garden crisscrossed by peddlers of balloons and biscuits, the child of old flew kites and rolled hoops with the daughters of Félix Faure, before he was President of the Republic.

In the Rue Boissy d'Anglas, Cocteau, Radiguet and their companions call a halt at Le Boeuf sur le toit, the meeting place *par excellence* of the Roaring Twenties – Proust had gone there to acquaint himself with jazz. After feasting on crêpes, they jump into a cab to arrive at Père-Lachaise cemetery before the others.

Thirteen months later, Raymond Radiguet will follow Proust to the grave. Then it will be the turn of Maurice Barrès and very shortly afterwards Anatole France, and Sarah Bernhardt, but they were no longer young.

At Père-Lachaise

Along the avenue, rising toward the Place Gambetta, there is nothing to be seen but undulating hills, the rounded back of the lawn, the towering trees. The worst is the Boulevard de Ménilmontant, deserted this high up, razed, gloomy, the immense gate of the Entrée principale at the end of Rue de la Roquette, which climbs from the Bastille, the route that all the funeral processions have pounded out on foot, past the locals, the shabby shops, families at the windows among the drying bedsheets, the incarcerated in the women's prison drinking in the noise of the crowd.

Up top, the wall looks as though it could mark the perimeter of a barracks or a prison, but with no surveillance. Paris no longer exists, it has become God knows what subprefecture of the back of beyond, a city of the dead. Interminable days, a life that will never end. Summer or winter, it is always November. The cold is glacial, the wind sweeps whistling between the plane trees.

Père-Lachaise itself does not much appreciate newcomers. All at once, the cemetery takes on the look of a construction site. Rubble, clods of soil dug up without any hope of finding hidden treasure, rickety boards above the trench.

Clinging to the rocky hillsides of the Peloponnesus,

little whitewashed tombstones overlook the violent blue of the sea. The flames of fat red candles flicker endlessly. A photo and a few trinkets are arranged inside a little display case that slides open at the head of the grave. Next to mementos of the dear departed, there are one or two glasses from which to drink the cool lemonade you brought with you, and a dust rag and a little bottle of household cleaner for upkeep.

Cemeteries really ought to be set deep in forests, amid meadows, in the middle of the watercourses in the Pré Catelan, or — as on San Michele, across the lagoon from Venice — on islands you can only reach on certain days, by ferry. Over there, the buildings look like file folders, bays of library shelving; they are as tiny as the disorderly graves in their enclosures. On Diaghilev's, ballet shoes have been strewn as offerings, dirty and mismatched ballet shoes.

A voice rings out over the loudspeaker, in the island's silence. A woman's voice from beyond the grave, a disembodied voice like that of Death or of the telephone operators in a distant past invites the visitor to leave. She proffers her message in four languages, tirelessly she repeats it into the void on a never-ending loop.

Mausoleums

The family vault is all the way at the top.

You had to climb the hill, to pass in front of innumerable sentry-boxes under the gaze of statues, to walk through the fallen leaves. Finally, at the entrance to the alleyway – 85th division, first row to the left of the path, two meters wide – a birdman stands guard. A family mausoleum memorializes in soft stone the energetic face of a young aviator killed in combat. An irony of fate: the hero's first name is Albert – whose equivalent in the weaker sex has always been, transparently, Albertine.

Beneath the carnival mask, isn't this Proust's little mechanic, his dear Albert Agostinelli, whom, among others, he had wished to dress as a woman, to stretch out forever on the paper bed? Some weeks before the declaration of war in 1914, Agostinelli (under the assumed name of Marcel Swann) had crashed his airplane into the depths of the Mediterranean. He scarcely knew how to fly. After divers had succeeded in bringing up the body in its rubber mantle, Proust, heartbroken, sent the family an astronomically expensive wreath – but they lamented that the flowers were not artificial, which would have reduced the cost of future maintenance.

Three steps farther on, here is the parents' tomb.

A simple slab of black marble shining like a mirror, appalling.

Today, a new stone has replaced the original. Mistaken one autumn night for the grave of a martyr sacrificed to the Armenian cause, whom it was thought best to kill a second time, the site was bombed some twenty years ago. Nobody wants to talk about it.

As for the slender tomb that rises opposite Proust's (to see it you have to turn around or, even better, adopt the angle of vision of the dead), in this season it is carpeted with green moss. And approaching it, you can decipher the name of these neighbors. Carved high up, to facilitate reading: here lies the 'Pages' family.

The Registry Office

An immense sign indicates in capital letters that smoking is prohibited. The minute the Registry Office opens, a cloud of gray tobacco smoke pollutes the air; the employees are dissecting last night's activities. Here is the epic poem of office life amid the files, the index cards, the registers. I was always calling too early or arriving too late. 'She's in the field,' I was invariably told, whenever I asked to speak with the only person who could tell me the secrets of the place. Long before, I had wanted to know everything about the tomb surmounted by skulls and little demons in which lay buried physicist and aeronaut Etienne-Gaspard Robertson, the inventor of the Phantasmagoria, who has been housed on Casimir-Perier Alley since 1837. What was the date of the grave's restoration (the cleansing of the stone had removed from the sarcophagus the aura of a Black Mass), when had the gigantic chestnut tree been planted, why did no other names appear, though inside the tomb twelve are buried?

This time, it was Proust who led me here. Proust? The writer? They could not give me any information, it was confidential. The point being that his burial site still had some rightful owners, a term loaded with red tape. For a fraction of a second, I envisioned his lineage, a swarm of young girls flitting through the bushes, their complexions still peaches-and-cream, their laughter cascading.

The Registry Office staff were in a muddle. But finally I found out, thanks to them, despite them, what I wanted to know: whether or not Proust was buried with both his parents. It had been claimed that only his mother was in the tomb, that Marcel, once dead, had her to himself, himself alone, that at last he had been able to assuage his ancient childhood sorrow, his only-son fantasy, those nights when his mother had abandoned him to join the guests in the living room.

They assured me that this was untrue, all the while persistently confusing the son with his father, whom they metamorphosed into a Greek hero: *Achille*, they kept on saying, meaning Adrien Proust (this French equivalent of Achilles was his second given name), Achille had been buried there since 1903. I held proof positive in my hands. A little typewritten yellow card specified that he who had had the awesome privilege, in the phrase necessitated by these circumstances, of inaugurating the site was indeed Professor Proust, physician in the hospitals of Paris, member of the Academy of Medicine, author of several treatises on hygiene (among them, *The Hygiene of the Neurasthenic*, which must have enthralled his son), joined by his wife two years later.

So once again, Marcel's father and mother had been

waiting for him. In fact, as their son had progressed through his trials and tribulations across Paris, they had never ceased to live with him as paintings hung in the living room of each of his successive residences, like the household gods of Antiquity.

The Image of his Mother

He is the spitting image of his mother. He has her eyes, people say tenderly, especially when Marcel plays at being awkward or ingenuous. The dead woman's eyes have been grafted onto her son's face, into the hollows of his eye sockets.

He looks at the world through her eyes, he makes her see what she never tried to see, what she never wanted to know.

Proust is said to have confessed that with his mother's death he had been tempted to let himself die. It was the consequences of his act, the prospect of committing – more than a crime – a matricide that changed his mind: for along with him, his memory of her would have perished. But who knows if bringing her back to life would not open her eyes too wide.

Reincarnations

He loved to play the game of likenesses. He identified the lookalikes among his contemporaries, the doubles of Victor Hugo, Louis Pasteur, Liane de Pougy, Sarah Bernhardt... He is always on the lookout for resemblances, reincarnations, sex changes, family secrets. He is insatiable, he lies in wait for incest, between sisters and brothers, mothers and sons.

When an unknown young man sends him a letter from Mayence, he immediately requests his photograph. He wants to see the look of this Jacques Benoist-Méchin, who has written to him; to find out whether he resembles his mother, whom Proust had known in the salons of the Faubourg Saint-Germain around 1895, twenty-five years earlier. But she whom he wants to see beneath her son's image, appearing like a watermark held up to the light — that woman is not, in fact, the boy's real mother. The young man has never even met her, for she was his father's first wife. This weighs on Benoist-Méchin's conscience, but if he confesses, he runs the risk of upsetting his correspondent and, worse yet, of losing all mystery, all attraction, in Proust's eyes.

So without comment, he sends a photo of himself in uniform, a snapshot taken on a boat ride along the Rhine by a fellow conscript (Robert Le Vigan, as it happens, who was then not yet an actor), an image like those in newspaper wedding announcements.

Proust thanks the young soldier warmly, struck of course by his astonishing resemblance to his 'mother.' At first, Benoist-Méchin enmeshes himself further into his deception, then finally, overcome by remorse, confesses the truth. The dreaded response reaches him at last in his barracks. Instead of being angry, Proust propounds to him his theory: sons are the material, physical echo of their father's erotic type − one could even say its developer, as in photography − unbound by the ties of biology or blood.

Prowler

I loathe the Père-Lachaise Cemetery, but I began returning to it. Mornings, evenings, lunchtimes, I took to lurking there, whether under drizzle or an intensely blue sky punctuated by the white streak of an airliner. Eventually the ghosts must let themselves be tamed; they would come out to meet me. 'We the living,' Proust wrote, 'we are all the dead who have not yet taken up our posts.'

I crossed paths with pilgrims, wanderers. I avoided routine, I came at different hours, I varied my route, changed tactics. Often I got lost, I was unable to retrace my steps. From dawn to dusk, sunrise to sunset, the light, but above all the sound, the noises are never the same. The worst of them border on terror, then imperceptibly you pass to the other side.

Theory of Ghosts

At the first glimmer of day, August Strindberg glides along the paths. In his closed fist, he carefully holds a little phial of liquefied lead acetate, which he gingerly carries from one grave to the next, 'like a bird catcher spared the effort of luring [his] prey.' This scene was played out toward the turn of the last century, in the Montparnasse Cemetery.

He is hunting souls – that is, dematerialized bodies – convinced that the foliage of elms and lime trees, roses, even putrefying, and the tears shed by all and sundry all exhale the fluid of the departed.

Strindberg did more than simply seek to wake the dead, to capture their presence beyond the tomb. Everywhere in his apartment, even in his study, he displayed photographic images of all his lost loved ones, life-sized faces, full-length portraits, enlargements with which he surrounded himself at the end of his life.

Like others who tried to record not just the visible form of human beings, but also the aura of their passions and impulses, Strindberg even claimed to photograph the invisible. His 'celestographs' are taken without a camera or lens, captured directly on the surface of the light-sensitive plate. They aim to photograph the soul, to make photography an instrument of divination, a medium.

Before him, and every bit as seriously, the 'optogram' had been devised. It was believed to be the ultimately unimpeachable instrument for identifying criminals. By scrutinizing, close-up, photographs of murder victims' retinas, one could reconstruct the very last image imprinted there, the fatal instant.

Such fads went hand in glove with the origins of the daguerreotype. Hadn't Balzac concocted his own physiology of photography, which he called the 'theory of ghosts'? So reported Félix Nadar, who had heard it from Balzac's own lips. Since every man consists of a series of superimposed ghosts, 'layered in infinitesimal strata,' successive photographic shots must inevitably strip away a layer at a time from the photographed individual.

A Family Photograph

We might dream of holding in our hands a few 'celestographs' of Proust, to borrow Strindberg's term. But it would no more have occurred to Céleste to snap a photo of her Monsieur Proust than to scribble notes or keep a journal, as her master had encouraged her to do. What could have possessed her to do such a thing?

As for Proust, might he himself, at least once in his life, have been a photographer?

This hypothesis is strongly supported by a photograph of Adrien Proust, the writer's father, in company with Robert Proust, the writer's brother. The two men stand on the balcony of a Parisian apartment house, brought into perspective by the vanishing and ethereal image of a wrought-iron railing that flees away from the viewer like a stone slide. In the sun-flooded void beyond it, we see the empty city at an even steeper angle because the road plunges almost vertically down to a crossroads with the ubiquitous Boulevard Haussmann (this is on the second floor of the modern eight-room apartment on the Rue de Courcelles to which Proust's parents had moved, just above the Place du Pérou).

The background might easily be taken for a canvas by Gustave Caillebotte, who in the 1880s often painted or photographed his confidants in front of the windows and balustrades of Haussmannian apartment houses.

Wedged behind his father, a man in his sixties, with salt-and-pepper beard, the younger son seems his very reflection, his successor in the prime of life. The black of both their suits stands out against the pale background; both assume an air of arrogance, of the self-satisfaction that comes with social success, of virile complicity (the father will soon marry off his son – quite sensibly – to his mistress's own daughter). They are two actors in a bourgeois allegory, a celebration of Time.

Adrien and Robert Proust have stepped outside to present themselves to the day. The light is dazzling at this hour, and behind them the shutters are closed, for fabrics and curtains must be protected from the effects of direct sunlight. At the behest of the unidentified photographer, the father has emerged from the living room and come through the French window onto the balcony. In one hand he still holds a newspaper, folded in two – the newspaper he must have been reading after lunch, or just before sitting down to table.

The two men are not looking directly at the camera, which they would have done instinctively if the picture had been taken with a pre-set timer. They are looking slightly to the right. Whoever is taking aim at them must be a close friend or family member. Professor Proust has not thought it necessary to remove the informal cap he wears when at home with his family. Is it likely that an outsider might receive such a mark of intimacy?

In addition, if a stranger to the domestic circle had photographed the scene, wouldn't this guest have had to take a second picture, perfectly symmetrical to the first? And this time wouldn't Marcel have been asked to come and replace his younger sibling? He would have joined his father and stood, in his turn, behind the head of the family. If this photograph does not exist, surely it must be because, just this once, Marcel played the role of photographer.

And to whom else would the camera belong but Robert? The 20th century is beginning. The young surgeon values anything modern, all the new technology. This is a Folding, which was easy to handle. Or – who knows? – maybe even a Ligier stereoscope, that little machine which, along with the invention of the cinema, will continue to vacuum-pack, so to speak, the whole era. Robert Proust set up the shots, he showed his brother how to proceed, then he stepped back to pose for the photograph, not without misgivings about the operation's success.

After contorting himself, for the balcony is narrow, the apprentice leaned for support against the blurry line at the center of the image: the railing above the city. Immediately afterwards, Robert must have offered to photograph Marcel, but the latter categorically refused. Light was too painful to him, and he'd already had more than he could bear.

At the end of the balcony on the Rue de Courcelles, it is Marcel at whom father and brother are looking forever, he is the absent one, whom we see, so alone, deep in their eyes.

Faces

Of Proust the adult, there exist at the very most twenty or so photographs. Except for those rare images taken at the very end of his life, these photos date exclusively from the period of the 1890s, after his military service, to the early 1900s, 1905 at the latest. They have imperceptibly conditioned us to see through youthful masks, sometimes frowning, sometimes smiling, always marked by melancholy, to an evolving Proust, presumably aging, but eternally true to himself.

Doesn't Proust seem – in his way of being and his self-presentation, in his physique and manner of dress, in the ideogram of his moustache – a kind of secret brother to those elegant comic actors who so amused the 1910s and '20s, indifferent to the catastrophes they unleashed in their wake?

Indeed, few of those who knew him well took him seriously. In retrospect, we think of this man who always spoke of *papa, maman,* never of *my father, my mother,* as an elderly spoiled child, and it is true that in his bedroom he threw everything on the floor as soon as he was done with it, papers, handkerchiefs, newspapers, objects.

Eventually, suffering from uremia, he gets puffy, but resembles a little baby, a fat schoolboy. Unanimously, everybody – his brother Robert, Léon Daudet, Barrès, his inner circle – calls him 'the poor little thing.'

Emmanuel Berl maintains that for Proust an old man was no more than a young man on whom age had imposed a wig, a beard, a fake nose, false wrinkles.

Whether out of a performer's coquetry or a refusal to appear in public, Proust does not in fact leave us any image of himself after the 1903–1905 period (as it happens, these are also the dates of the deaths of his parents, before he begins to write his novel).

In May of 1921, Proust reappears in the developing tray. Three snapshots are taken of him, most probably in the early afternoon, in front of the esplanade of the Jeu de Paume, with the help of a little Vest Pocket Kodak that Jean-Louis Vaudoyer, who accompanied him to the Tuileries, must have brought along with him.

This is when the last photograph, the best-known, was taken: he stands as straight as he can, a martial silhouette, holding his cane like a saber. He resists the atmospheric pressure with all his strength, he fills his lungs before taking flight. The other two photos are closer shots of his face and bust: wing collar, ample cravat hastily knotted. In one of them, Proust closed his eyes in the instant when the shutter clicked, and in the second, from which the leafy background has disappeared, obscured by cloudy white, the somewhat low angle of the shot accentuates the ecstatic set of his features. His gaze is open this time, but empty, absent, deep circles under his eyes, the lower part of his face swollen, while his jacket, suffering from discoloration, seems already tarnished with verdigris.

By comparison, it is in the deathbed portraits taken at the Rue Hamelin that Proust seems more alive, absorbed by the final sleep, shielded from his dreams.

Ex-voto

The tangle of dates, last names, first names, the layers of memory, the precipices of forgetfulness, the sufferings, absences, jealousies, emotions slowly building, all of it floods in, all the destinies in brief, the succinct destinies summed up in encrypted messages, in tender words almost effaced, in treasure troves of black humor.

The masterpieces of commemorative statuary are perhaps of a kind with the most ridiculous ex-votos. At the summit of the steps inside Santa Maria dei Frari, the door of the dazzling pyramid which is Canova's tomb remains open. Here, on one square of the giant hopscotch board, Madame Raspail's face is no more than a draped cloth mingling with stone. Only her naked, languid arm clings like ivy to the slit window of the dungeon into which her husband has been thrown. You might mistake her for a larger-than-life statue of Céleste.

Balzac, Gérard de Nerval, Champollion, Gustave Doré, and Charles Nodier, and Nadar, and Apollinaire, then Méliès and Raymond Roussel, and Reynaldo Hahn, whose voice was so tender when he sang of the sky so blue, so calm… Indians whose ancestors had been buried went to dig them up after dark, in an immemorial rite, transferring them into caves so they would not be tired out by the weight of the earth.

Even though Proust lies surrounded by good company, his days spent underground must seem interminable. What does he dream about on certain evenings? Tender Fates, angels with vacant gazes, eternal fiancés, tearful mothers, plaster masks, marble faces, faded photographs, cheap relics. The glass trinkets fall to pieces, but the diadems remain forever in flower. Under every funerary slab, there are keys. Under every stone, there is a haunted house.

Who could possibly read, by means of a few letters carved in stone, the extraordinary secrets of a line of descent, and all the impossibles loves? Names that we decipher, names that we spell out, beings whom we name are reborn on our lips, and wandering souls at last find their burial place.

Rather than raising roofs over them, we should thrust aside the mortuary slabs, pillage the tombs, crouch over the dead, all of them contemporaries, identify each of the ghosts pressed up against each other, practice palmistry, metempsychosis, the invocation of ancestral spirits, the resurrection of bodies.

Who would not wish to put the flesh back on these whitened bones, and then the blood, the breath, the gaze, the dimple in the chin, the ringlets, the beauty marks that are the spice of life, and what tenderness it takes to slip the sleeping beauties a taste of magic potion without breaking the spell.

This is our Egypt, this is our Pompeii. Like the tombstones in the Jewish cemetery in Prague, all in disorder amid the clouds of crows like ink pearled at the tip of the quill, each of these steles is the page of an open book. A book into which we might walk, slipping between the walls and down the corridors, advancing with a light step to pass through the invisible.

Immense Rebus

No eulogy was pronounced. But the condolence line stretches out forever.

If he had still possessed the eyes to see it all and ears to hear, the deceased would have had the time of his life. Didn't Picasso, who had met Proust a few months earlier at Étienne de Beaumont's New Year's Eve party, immediately see through him, a true connoisseur: 'Take a look! He's copying from real life!'

The funeral procession, which resembles an anthill, a cavalcade of insects, forms an immense rebus. The whole tribe is present, all his models in a jumble, arms, legs, hands, smiles, gestures, tears, heads, outer shells. All the dismembered bodies that Bluebeard cut and pasted in his den to form their doubles, their puppets: Gilberte, Swann, Odette de Crécy, the Guermantes, the Verdurins, Saint-Loup, Morel, Elstir, Vinteuil, Cottard, the Baron de Charlus, and even Albertine, the model little girls and Miss Sacripants, the Queens of the Carnaval, the ladies of easy virtue who believe themselves Madame Bovary, the professional mourners, the muses, the tomboys and the bad boys, the young girls in flower and the sleeping beauties.

Trophies

Armed with a swan-feather fan, the Countess Greffuhle appears in a cloud of muslin, dressed by Worth in black velvet strewn with white lilies or costumed as Notre Dame de Thermidor; Madame Aubernon appears as a Valkyrie, like Marie de Benardaky, as Minerva like the Marquise d'Hervey de Saint-Denis; and then here is Mrs. Standish (whom he observed from his window when he lived on Rue Hamelin), the Princess Bibesco, Henri Greffuhle, the blond-bearded ogre disguised as Jupiter or Golo, of course Robert de Montesquiou, Laure Hayman, Madeleine Lemaire, Laure de Sade, that is, the Countess de Chevigné, who because she found them too verbose and they cluttered up her drawers, lost or burned most of the letters with which her admirer never ceased to shower her. The same one who wrote to her (it was at the end, he had moved out definitively): 'I had heart attacks every time I met with you…'

Family albums, card collections, photos of friends, photos of his cherished idols, the images shimmering with gelatin silver bromide, were pledges, trophies. A fetishist of matter, it was as though he had to extract specimens from the ambient world as tangible proof, primarily for his own eyes, that he had not invented everything. He had had to tear these little photos from their owners' grasp, to snatch them from their subjects. It was a treasure that he had amassed in his lair, his darkroom.

He must have performed miracles to become the owner of all these chemical bodies, these figurines, these exorcist's effigies, these icons. The daughters' images replace those he could never get from their mothers. He had to wait for seven years, seven years of sorrow, before Robert de Rothschild finally gave him, one evening at the Ritz in 1922, a little calling card belonging to his dear Bertrand de Fénelon, killed at the front in early winter 1915.

Ink has no odor, but images do. We see Proust's shadow cast over all these glossy photographs. We hear his breathing, sense his pulsing blood, his hands. He has all the men and women who swan across these pieces of cardboard at his mercy. But these bodies so carefully clothed, these good souls whom he hides in his bureau drawer, doesn't he spend his time skinning them, stripping them naked? He wants to see what is beneath, as in the collections of 'curious' or 'oriental' photographs sold under the counter: wasp waists, flesh, meat, fat, postures, harem exotica, two-bit enchantments.

Glacial Cold

For once, when you arrive at his apartment, Céleste fails to sniff you out.

The bedroom is as glacial as a tomb. Despite the bitter cold, he had forbidden a fire in the fireplace for fear of suffocating, for fear of being asphyxiated. Marcel Proust liked to repeat to Léon Daudet's younger brother, Lucien, the diagnosis given by the pulmonologist he often consulted: 'I could perhaps cure your asthma, but I do not want to. Given the degree to which you are asthmatic, and the form your asthma takes, it serves as an outlet, it spares you other illnesses…'

In the vestibule, in the living room whose furniture is draped with dust covers, stricken visitors are whispering. The whole apartment resembles a burglarized villa, an abandoned house. His friends are dumbstruck: they file through his dressing room at an hour when they would never, ever have been admitted. Suddenly they flout all etiquette, the utmost protocols of the laws of hospitality.

Gliding Like an Ice Skater

Gliding in like an ice skater when he arrived at salons late, wandering voluptuously through the world, white camellia in his buttonhole, spruce and 'pimped up' (the French term used to describe him, *pimponné*, was obviously invented by Fargue, mixing the adjective *pimpant* [smart] with the verb *pomponner* [to doll up]) to the point of being highly irritating with his bowings and scrapings, his poutings.

Everyone has a go at describing him:

Eyes of black, piercingly intelligent eyes of velvet, doe eyes, eyes shining and circled in the yellowish-brown of insomnia, heavy eyelids, curly beard that will ultimately swallow his face, the look of an El Greco painting, a Neapolitan prince, an Assyrian magus, the little Chaplinesque mustache, the freshly shaved cheeks like a fruit or vegetable ripened in the cellar, the pallid skin, his flesh almost transparent, the fringe deep black over his forehead, his hair as stiff and shiny as if he had polished it, his teeth whiter than white.

Ghosts are invoked, and pleasures and days.

All those who knew him mention his generosity: his tips are astronomical, he does not rest until his friends are happy, he mediates, he helps out, he ruins himself buying flowers and charming gifts, he is prepared to spend 27,000 francs (in 1914) to purchase an airplane for his little chauffeur, to buy him a Rolls, and still he fails to win his heart.

With his family gone, he transfers his need for consolation onto the world into which he sometimes descends: he begs for people to take care of him, to love him more, he turns on the charm, he banters, he is all sweetness and light, he flatters the whole world, he plunges freely into the vanity fair.

He forgets his gloves everywhere, sends interminable gifts and letters pleading that they be returned, offers new ones in exchange for the old. He is praised for the extreme courtesy of his speech, the refinement of his manners (his schoolmates had mockingly invented the verb 'to proustify'), his sweetness, his modesty, his vivacious spirit.

At every turn, he says 'perhaps.'

Fit of Laughter

Anna de Noailles cannot forget how his deep and sorrowful gaze would abruptly brim with malice, with a bubbling-up of laughter. And Jean Hugo can still see the downcast, almost supplicating eyes suddenly begin to sparkle like champagne. The writer was incapable of reading even a few pages of his book-in-progress to his friends without being seized by a fit of laughter, a nervous laugh that forced him to stop.

This was because of how he had been brought up. 'Mister Member-of-the-Académie-Française,' his father used to call him, as a joke. And his mother, who adored teasing him, was not to be outdone. When he was thirteen, his schoolteacher of Natural Sciences led a double life. Under the pseudonym of Christophe, he was the author of the satirical series *The Fenouillard Family*.

Proust's sense of humor came with a gift for imitation. He satirizes everything he gets his hands on, he even caricatures the Dreyfusards, despite being one himself. He mimics the ageing Anatole France as though it were second nature to him, unleashing in triplicate the paradoxical epithets he so enjoyed. This, despite the fact that Proust has always respectfully called him 'Monsieur France.' He simulates the groans of Robert de Montesquiou (at whose feet he so long pretended to kneel), his scoldings, his squeals reproduced to perfection.

When in the mood, he greets his visitors with Paris street cries: 'Gla-zier! Gla-zier!…'

To delight him, all you have to do is reply:
'Ah mesdames, voilà du bon fromage
Il est du pays de celui qui l'a fait
Celui qui l'a fait, il est de son village
Ah, Mesdames, voilà du bon fromage.'
(*Ah ladies, this cheese is good*
It's from the same place as the fellow who made it
The fellow who made it is from his village
Ah, ladies, this cheese is good!')

He has always had a weakness for the music hall. He loves Fragson, the *Caf' conc'*, the ditties of Mayol; unhesitatingly he hums 'Come, Sweetheart.'

When Bouls-ni-Bouls (the nickname of Proust's cherished Reynaldo Hahn) pays a visit, he lands directly at the foot of Marcel's bed, via the hall door, disregarding the stops imposed on visitors, the circuit of antechambers, and he remains standing, he's a breath of fresh air, always very elegant, very funny, very bitchy, very intimate. The composer of Verlaine's *Gray Songs* is dressed up as a favourite of Henri III. Could he be one of the precious few to address Proust as 'tu'?

The two friends bill and coo, fence with each other, delight in aggressive witticisms, bawdy stories, exchange pot-shots and flowers. Reynaldo comes to lay at Marcel's feet the bounty of his evening, the feast of Paris Society. Their imitations are shadow puppets that jostle on the walls in the candlelight.

Everything Interests Him

Arms crossed over his chest, his left hand supporting his right elbow, he filters everything he says through his other hand, speaking through the fingers that play in front of his mouth.

He listens, he gossips. He is an incurable snob. He revels in the stories of the aristocracy; the Second Empire shines more brightly than any fairy tale (this is also the golden age of Félix Nadar's photography studio). Solid citizens and the bourgeoisie are completely without romance, they are too afraid of their own madness; the most interesting families hail from the House of Atreus.

He is deeply curious about everything that does not directly involve him, but everything involves him, for he is of the chameleon species. He knows all there is to know, idle rumors, gossip, genealogical trees, the history of every church tower in Île-de-France. If he is stuck for a precise term or a colloquial phrase, he sends out ultimatums. He must have, by return mail, by *pneumatique*, by taxi, the exhaustive list of the contents of a young lady's needlework basket, the name of every rural railway line, the origin of the print on a Fortuny fabric, the exact rules governing the Japanese game of floating origami.

He wants to leave nothing to chance, he goes through

everything with his own fine-tooth comb. His memory is phenomenal. He reads the *Bottin mondain,* encyclopedias, train schedules, Balzac, Flaubert, Alexandre Dumas, Stevenson, Saint-Simon of course; he can recite *The Flowers of Evil* or complete monologues from Racine's tragedies, even verses by Sully Prudhomme. In real life, he prefers the company of Jean Béraud, Paul César Helleu or Jacques-Émile Blanche to the work of Degas or Cézanne, which he admits to not knowing well, that is, not much appreciating. But in his novel he is inspired by Renoir and Monet, although he does not know the art movements shaking up the new century, the Cubists and Fauves, nascent realism. He knows virtually by heart all of Wagner's operas, but he goes to see *Parade,* which caused a scandal. He admires Laurence Sterne, though *Tristram Shandy* is a reproach to just how far he did not go: writing his autobiography at the risk of his book, since only in its ninety-eighth chapter does the author at last recount the moment of his birth.

The News

He was born in the month following the *Semaine sanglante* that ended the Paris Commune. As a child, therefore, he must have leafed through the souvenir albums which had finally been authorized, the books as beautifully bound as if for a first communion, the softcover catalogues that inventoried the spectacle of devastation, the metaphors of carnage: buildings destroyed and burned, sacked churches, boulevards without paving stones, houses without roofs, rubble, debris, Paris in ruins.

In 1900, he flees from the World's Fair, which for several months transforms the west side of Paris into a stage set. Rather than gliding in a bateau-mouche down the short-lived Street of Nations, with its papier-maché pagodas, minarets and castles, he is in Venice. Without even considering the Basilica of San Marco, the canals and palaces are more magical and much truer mirages. The city seems entirely flooded, as Paris will be, later, during the great flood of the Seine.

But to begin his day, he must read all the newspapers. He follows the news, often ahead of his contemporaries. During the Dreyfus Affair, that cancer which ate away at every family (his own included) in France, '*et pas chez les Apaches*,' as he will recall, he is one of the first to side with the Dreyfusards. He does not miss a single court session in the trial of Émile Zola and finds it to be the happiest time in his life. His legend grows to such proportions that it is said as far away as Vienna (it is Stefan Zweig who tells Joseph Roth) that Proust has fought several duels to defend Captain Dreyfus's honor… The day when the first comic-opera railroad trains leave the heart of France for the Eastern frontiers, he is among the very few people who have a premonition of horror. 'Millions of men are going to be massacred in a war of the worlds comparable to that invented by Wells,' he writes in a letter on August 2nd, 1914, from deep within his bedroom.

One O'clock in the Morning

One o'clock in the morning, a June night, 1922. In a sky-blue uniform, on leave for an evening in Paris, a soldier, second class, in the French Army of the Rhine presents himself at a hotel reception desk. He is submitting to the conditions dictated by the Master. He is the one who sent his photograph, he is Jacques Benoist-Méchin (twenty years later he would narrowly escape ending his career in a closet in the Eagle's Nest at Berchtesgaden, accompanying Admiral Darlan to meet Hitler, but that's another story), he is twenty-one years old.

He is led into a scene colored pink by a taffeta lampshade. The air is heavy with benzoin resin and niaouli oil. The walls are covered with purple watered silk. It takes several seconds for the eyes to adjust.

Marcel Proust emerges from the gloom. Stretched out on a sofa, half-covered with a plaid throw-rug, he is wearing a tuxedo, his hands gloved in gray. Having come to discuss music, the young music lover must answer a series of questions from the writer, who in his ivory tower ponders the social, political, military situation in Germany. The informant talks, but we know nothing of what was really troubling his host.

Then Proust speaks of his defeat – a word the young Benoist-Méchin will not soon forget. For Marcel, this means he has finally decided that the last volume of *La*

Recherche will be called *Le Temps retrouvé* (Time Regained) instead of the title he had originally intended and which had been announced in the first volume published by Grasset: *L'Adoration perpétuelle* (Perpetual Adoration). 'There is no enduring ecstasy,' he murmurs, sending off his young guest.

Outside the door, the corridor of the Ritz is dimly illuminated by a night-light – just like the entrance to the Pharoah's room in the pyramids, notes Benoist-Méchin. In the Valley of the Kings, at this time, an archeologist is continuing his excavation of the riverbank facing Luxor.

On November 4th, 1922, Howard Carter uncovers a stone staircase buried in the sand, whose steps lead to the door of a tomb. It has remained sealed, and the room behind it will prove to be full of statues, beds, chairs, chests, weapons, urns, paintings. Proust will never know that the funeral chamber contained the sarcophagus of young Tutankhamun.

Unpredictable

He schedules his midnight rendezvous on the red banquettes at Chez Larue, at the Crillon, the Ritz. The little private room where he arranges to be served is a veritable furnace.

When he gives suppers, he moves from one guest to the next in turn, taking his plate with him. He delights in bringing together people who can't stand each other: Abel Hermant (who insulted the army), Anatole France (patriot, but Dreyfusard), Léon Daudet (who thought Captain Dreyfus a traitor). He loves to make trouble.

With him, you can never be sure what tomorrow will bring. He has the air of a d'Artagnan. His ripostes are biting, he is a fickle friend, he can easily take offense and become savage, furious, insolent. His sensitivity, his unpredictability, his endless grievances are legendary. Once, he threw his bedroom slippers in the face of a nuisance – and yet he is still a creature of the greatest delicacy. He puts up smokescreens. He is attracted to heartbreakers, he detests being 'feminine.' He is a tyrant who collects vows, pacts, reproaches.

A few words of advice: never ask him questions, never interrupt him, never mention what time it is or what the weather is outside, answer him in few words (and he will take your measure by them).

Out of Time

When he is expected for a visit, you can never know if he will actually show up. His household keeps his host's staff under siege, updating them every half-hour on how the preparations – that is, his successive delays – are progressing.

If he ever arrives, his convoluted sentences are clogged with irrelevant details, a muddle of excuses. Nonetheless, he is welcomed like a great explorer, a hero.

He is swallowed up in a long fur cloak too big for him, which he never takes off: 'he seemed to have arrived in his own coffin,' remembers Princess Bibesco. At his brother Robert's wedding, on February 2nd, 1903 at Saint-Augustin, he is zombie-like as he takes the collection alongside his cousin Valentine. Looking like a bridegroom or best man who had lost his wedding party (in fact he hated his friends getting married), there was something out of place, ridiculous about him. He was seen stumbling along in shoes that must no longer have fitted him, he was seen wearing his tie crooked or with his cuffs on backwards, he was seen badly dressed, his detachable collar threadbare or his gloves none too clean, his hair sticking up in tufts (and it is true that he sometimes fell prey to a sudden urge to trim his hair with nail scissors).

Stuffed into his collars, his dickey bulging, the arch of his spine even more accentuated by clothes that were too tight — his evening dress dated from another era — he gave the impression that he did not live in the present, but had fallen behind by one or two generations, in the backwaters of the past, a past he was unable to leave, under pain of death.

Time is a tunnel. Great families, bearers of illustrious names, supply the oxygen. Under the presidency of Poincaré, the height of elegance is to be able to cite remarks made two centuries before by Louis XV or one of his courtiers. While Proust waits for the dead to rise, while he bends over the balcony of his youth, while he scrutinizes projected images of days gone by, he does not see time passing. The women of the Roaring Twenties wear boys' haircuts, their skin is tan these days, they display their naked backs and their freckles, they are intoxicated by the tango and Black music.

False Dandy

This dandy had every opportunity to be idle; idleness is a virtue in his class. If pressed, he might have written pointless poems and published two or three cloth-bound pamphlets, a few sparse pieces of art criticism in *Le Figaro* (and this he did).

But Proust is a workaholic, his nose to the grindstone, working himself to death. Living on a private income does not prevent him from throwing money out the window. He plays the market, he speculates. But the more years that pass, the riskier his investments become; and the more overwhelming his financial worries, the more he complains, the more avid he is for easy schemes, the more money-grubbing, increasingly incapable of compromise – especially in his role as a man of letters. Just as the accursed writer continually hired typists, stenographers, secretaries, assistants, so too he micromanaged the rollout of his work, oversaw and negotiated its publication, parceled out the *work in progress* to appear in the form of extracts, blocks, lots.

Being consumed by his book does not prevent him from plotting the sale of all the armchairs he has warehoused in his apartment, the mahogany tables, the carpets, the sideboards, the couches, the bronzes. A certain Monsieur Dubois ultimately takes on the job, and does it very ineptly despite his last name, as

Céleste says, proud as she is to have succeeded in saving a crystal chandelier (you'd think you were in a Molière play). Some of the family furniture even ends up at Albert Le Cuziat's establishment. It was later found at the bathhouse for gentlemen of which the aforementioned Le Cuziat was the manager, and is thought to have been furnished by Proust in person.

No matter the circumstances, he is conscious that there are some more needy than he. In 1917, he offers his services to his friend Marie Scheikévitch, stripped of her fortune by the Russian Revolution, famous in Paris for having failed in a suicide attempt and invented in minute detail a love affair with Anatole France. To this woman, lovelorn but of a beautiful disposition, her skin so white that men thought her made of paper, he proposed in all seriousness that he become her ghost writer in the newspaper *Le Temps*, writing daily under her name 'minor news items, but better.'

It's Temporary

The elevator ascends, trembling, to the fifth floor. The apartment is a replica of the one on Boulevard Haussmann, but in a slightly reduced size. He has requisitioned the floor beneath his, but he tells anyone who will listen that he is living in a squalid hovel.

It is temporary, he is camping out, he still hopes to move. The huge sheets of cork are being kept in a garage, and the whole apartment resembles a storage unit. This is nothing compared to his former dining room, which people used to enter as though penetrating the heart of a forest – it had been condemned to hold his bric-a-brac, the alluvia of inheritances.

No more grand piano, mirrored wardrobe, nor chest of drawers in his bedroom, but still the little Chinese cabinet that he so loved, and the low armchair for visitors. The room is bathed in the blue light coming through its satin curtains, and in the diffuse green glow of the singed shade of his bedside lamp.

The Bedroom

A magnificent overcoat with a black-and-white checked lining serves as his dressing gown: not because it is too worn — it was custom-made during his mother's lifetime at the 'Carnaval de Venise' near the Opéra — but because he is used to it. He cannot bear new clothes. Never would he have slept for two nights in the same sheets, yet he detests change in all things.

He is at one with his dwelling.

His three bedside tables have been transported to form a promontory beside his copper bed, and it is out of the question that the placement of anything might be changed.

On the two levels of the first bedside table, which is made of bamboo, he puts the books he is currently reading, the hot-water bottles he calls his 'boules,' and always a little mountain of handkerchiefs (but absolutely never newly bought handkerchiefs, for those are not delicate enough, not soft enough for his fragile skin).

The second table, made of walnut, is for the coffee tray (which, between certain hours, must always be at the ready), the nightly herbal tea, the bottle of Evian water (a new one every day, despite the fact that he never drinks a mouthful).

On the third, an antique rosewood drop leaf table,

there is his bottle of ink, his pen holder, and his supply of Sergent Major pens, his watch and all his pairs of eyeglasses (he has ten or twelve).

Beside his bedside lamp are his writing pads, his notebooks, the accordion of pasted-together sheets of paper. The thirty-two black notebooks with moleskin covers, said to be numbered by hand. The first versions of the manuscript, which had to remain always within reach, disappeared, it is said, into the kitchen stove at Boulevard Haussmann as he ceased to need them.

At the Theatre

As a young adolescent, Marcel had asked his Greek professor if he thought that he, Proust, would write for the theatre when he grew up – would he one day be performed at the Comédie-Française?

Upon his death, a friend comes to slip a ring belonging to his mother onto the writer's finger. This was a cameo which Anatole France, at the end of the premiere of his play *The Red Lily*, gave to its leading lady, the great Réjane.

This friend, Réjane's son, will never forget his discovery of Proust, years earlier. He recounts how, returning home one evening, he found a lady waiting for him in the vestibule of his apartment. Dressed like one of the provincial women in a bourgeois novel, she was smiling the fixed smile of a sculpted angel. This was Céleste – without whom life would have been 'an insoluble problem' for Marcel.

With circumlocutions that owed everything to the mannerisms of her master, she explained to Réjane's son that, touched by what he had said about *Du côté de chez Swann* – five years earlier, incidentally – Proust had asked mutual friends to introduce them to each other, and that since these friends had done nothing, her master had resolved to send Céleste herself with an invitation to come visit him. But Proust's extraordinary courtesy allowing for no opposition, she added: 'Monsieur Prouste [Céleste added a final 'e' everywhere], begging your pardon, insists that Monsieur Porel come see him, on Boulevard Haussmann, tomorrow evening, at eleven o'clock.'

Hallucination

Visits always take place in the middle of the night. They are waking dreams, visions that he stages, hallucinations.

'After the wait,' as Paul Morand, for his part, describes it, 'we are introduced into the bedroom. Proust, rolled up in his long cloak, wearing a morning coat and gray suede shoes, with cane, gloves of pearl gray, too tight, as in Manet's paintings, which give him wooden hands; his face delicate and sweet, encroached on at the temples by black hair, the heavy chin buried in his collar, high cheekbones, tormented ears, an air of being sicker than ever, yellow, back bent, chest sunken. A bottle of champagne and two flutes on a little side table. Proust tried to stand up but felt ill. He leaves us, to return to his bed.'

Being in bed is his natural state. Seated, he always looks uncomfortable, contorted, twisted, coiled, robotic.

The Paper Bed

He knits in bed, he unravels and darns his sentences, his pages, he moves them around, rearranges them, cuts and tightens them up.

Despite asthma attacks, physical exhaustion, his own obstinate refusal to take care of himself, the author dedicates his life and every last bit of his energy to finishing *La Recherche*, continuing to write and write, leaving the mark of his impatience in missing words, empty spaces to be filled in later. He corrects typescripts by hand, he corrects proofs with corrections that must be corrected in their turn. (The printer must decipher them himself; the copyeditors let innumerable typos through. The one in charge of rereading *Le Côté de Guermantes* is no better than the others. His name is André Breton.)

He writes lying on his back, like Michelangelo painting the ceiling of the Sistine Chapel. He writes with the paper on his knees, without a lap desk, without anything. He writes only in bed, buried amidst his disordered sheets of paper, the thousands of letters he sends out, the swollen notebooks of his manuscript, the backs of envelopes, the reverse sides of prescriptions or bills strewn with sentences, the famous *paperoles*, glued-together rolls of paper, the newspapers heaped on the sheets. He writes submerged in paper like a shroud.

Vigil

Between Saturday the 18th and Wednesday the 22nd of November, Céleste refuses to believe it. 'My God,' she murmurs, 'please let him say something to me.'

Céleste would like a miracle, like Lazarus's sister whose hair shone with ointment of spikenard. She waits at the end of the bed, she keeps watch until the fourth day.

His eyes no longer devour visitors.

His black beard, remarked upon by everyone, his vacation beard, his old sea-dog beard, his ragpicker beard – we see it only in the deathbed portraits, never in any of the photos taken while he was alive.

His face floats above the white sheets.

He is a drowned man descending the current, a head liberated from its body, detached from its torso like the head of Saint John the Baptist, which Salomé offered Herodias on a bronze platter.

The Flood of Portraitists

In keeping with Proust's last wishes – they had known each other in Cabourg – or perhaps at the insistence of his brother Robert, here comes Paul-César Helleu to paint the portrait of the deceased. It is Jacques Porel who goes to fetch the artist, nicknamed by Degas 'the steam-driven Watteau,' so speedily did he turn out pictures of 'Femmes-Lianes.'

Helleu works in drypoint for two hours. The artificial light bouncing off the large copper surface hurts his eyes, 'but how beautiful he was!' Helleu relates. 'He was beautiful, we should have molded a death mask.' After being inked and pulled, the plate, one meter across, will invert the image of Proust, as if, to see him better, the viewer had managed to move to the other side of the bed, as if the far wall had somehow been folded away. There are two versions. In the first, the face is shaggy, wrapped up in bed linens. In the second – the first portrait retouched? – the black beard and hair are clearly outlined, and the chin is free of the sheets, raised out of the bed.

The day Proust won the Goncourt prize ('that publicity machine,' he grumbled, when in fact he had pulled off an unbelievable surprise attack, supported by Léon Daudet's covering fire, to triumph – *in extremis*, in December 1919, one year after the Armistice! – over

Roland Dorgelès' *The Wooden Crosses*), that day of the Goncourt, not one photographer, not one journalist had managed to penetrate his cell in Rue Hamelin. But today, and for three days running, what a crowd!

Dunoyer de Segonzac (a friend of Dorgelès, who made several etchings for his war novel) appears at the door. He does not know Proust; he has been dispatched by the *NRF*. He wishes to do several ink sketches. His five wash drawings are in very smooth ink, with scarcely a change in angle and only a few minuscule variations, slightly closer up or further away, except for one full frontal view of the face with longish hair. A certain Jean-Bernard Eschemann also stopped by. Paul Morand captured Proust with a stroke of his pen, and was so disturbed as to date the portrait wrong. The sculptor Robert Wlérick drew, somewhat clumsily, a leaden-faced profile.

More at home with the Dadaists or Paul Poiret's fashion models, Man Ray was roused from sleep to go and photograph 'a great writer,' in the words of a decidedly animated Cocteau. From Montparnasse, Man Ray hurries to the scene with all his equipment. A brief history of photography sums up Proust's life: Nadar *fils* immortalized the child, and then, when all was over, Man Ray appeared. He is not the only one: we know of three other photographs, attributed to Emmanuel Sougez, which rather resemble police mug shots. Paul Morand also reported having taken one last image of his friend, but at the printing, he let the negative burn.

The Reader's Way

A naked woman has fallen asleep stretched out on a couch. She has lost consciousness of herself, her extended arm still holds a book, the novel that has plunged her into the waters of night. Might this pink-fleshed woman in Félix Valloton's *The Reader* or *Reading Abandoned* – might this woman, sculpted sleeping in broad daylight, be the one who makes palpable to us the breath, the moist skin of the fugitive, Albertine, *disparue?*

Interior, Woman Reading

No, he was never in love, nor did he really have friends, avers Céleste, who, when she thinks of her past, cries out: 'It wasn't just the nights that were enchanted.'

Proust strongly encouraged her, she claimed, to keep a journal. She knows him better than anyone, no one knows better than she who he is, what he does, what he says. One must think of the future (and in fact she will survive him for more than half a century): after his death, the secrets he has confided to her will far outsell *Swann, Guermantes, Sodom et Gomorrhe,* and the rest. Just the thought of reversing their roles must have filled him with joy: she the writer, he the model; his life – his most quotidian, most ordinary life – the subject of her book.

Interior, Woman Reading: Caillebotte's canvas displays a woman seated in an armchair or lounge chair, all her attention on the newspaper she holds. Studying the image, we notice a man beneath the screen of the newspaper, a man deep within the painting, as though he were the very product of her reading, stretched out on the sofa behind her with a book in his hands, a miniaturized man, shrunk by the deformation of perspective, by an accelerated change in scale, a man lying down, engulfed by cushions. A dwarf almost like the principal of the boarding school in *Zero for Conduct*, played in Jean Vigo's film by a child glued into a false beard. When our gaze returns from the vanishing point, the woman in the foreground, who dominates the canvas, appears even more colossal.

True or false 'widows,' in the theater of the posthumous life of their great men, alter the genealogical order. As wives, even putative wives, they always end up playing the dual role of child and mother by becoming child-mothers.

From Morning to Evening

At the extendable table in his little dining room, Mallarmé recounted how he had seen a vastly popular show in a London music hall. A strange play: not a drama, not vaudeville, it had no subject and nothing even seemed to happen in it; a couple simply came to spend their evening in public.

Paul Valéry, who must have heard the story at one of Mallarmé's Tuesdays on the Rue de Rome, never forgot it. Late in life, he began to envision a film: a film, he confided, that he would have liked to make himself.

The screenplay would have been reduced to its simplest elements. You would have seen what happens to ordinary people in the course of an entire, uneventful day… And perhaps in this way you would have succeeded in making the interior of the characters show through, their exteriors like the transparent casings of certain insects in scientific documentaries.

Céleste Appears

Everything that he and Céleste do together is a ritual. At the signal, the ringing of the bell, she appears.

She spends her days in the little room beside the kitchen, waiting. She does almost nothing (never the cooking, in any case, but that was the contract they made: he hired her because she did not know how to do anything). She does not read; she waits for the bell. She remains on the alert, scrutinizing the semaphore system that connects the two sealed rooms in which they are each shut away. She must decipher every sign emitted by her patient, no matter how subtle: his silences, his absent gaze, his notes on scraps of paper, on the leaves that serve to light the Legras powder for fumigations. She knows his routines by heart.

Céleste came into his life in 1913, as the first volume of *La Recherche* was published. She was twenty-two, twenty years his junior. She was the one who ran his errands around Paris, explored by carriage the fashionable districts (they were like the New World to this child of Lozère), oversaw the sending of review copies, served as his press office, followed the scripts dictated by her invisible employer. But she was not authorized to wrap packages, nor to fold the colored papers, pink or blue depending on the gender of the addressee, nor even to tie up the packages with ribbons or pieces of string – like the one that fastened the manuscript sent to Rue Madame, to the *NRF*, which André Gide, it is said, never untied.

When Proust goes out Céleste waits up for him, no matter the hour. Her life resumes when he is present, but it is for her, moved or laughing, that he recounts his evenings. 'That way he had of bringing me the theater of the outside world and displaying it for me,' she says. 'It was as if he wanted to grasp Time by the hair to keep it from escaping and carrying away his characters.'

Céleste has the languid grace of a Modigliani.

During all those years spent in a state of high alert, on the set of their chamber play, she alternates the roles of whipping boy and perfect housewife. Together they perform *Little Red Riding Hood* or *Hansel and Gretel* or *The Arabian Nights*. This is a life of luxury: she goes to bed at dawn, she never gets up before noon. She sleeps in, every day. Time is no longer divided into hours, time is outside of time. Much later, the beautiful captive he was tyrannizing will say from the heart: 'With him, on the one hand life was ruled like music paper, but on the other, there was always the unexpected.'

Flesh and Blood

An extremely rare occurrence: she entered his book alive, as herself. Here is Céleste Albaret in the flesh, pure and unadorned. Like an apparition.

Not content to appear in camouflage (Françoise is her stand-in, as well as that of others), Céleste has the privilege of being, though so fleetingly that we wonder if we've imagined it, an actual character in the novel, giving her name to a character named, like her, Céleste Albaret.

A sure sign of affectionate complicity. The proof: all mentions of Céleste's name in Proust's text were added at the last minute, like the final codicil in a will. In fact, when in his list of the etymologies of plants Professor Brichot derives the patronym 'Albaret' from the name 'aubier' (sapwood) and the narrator whispers parenthetically, 'I must tell Céleste,' the wink is explicit. But Céleste is more than simply a proper name. By an irony of fate, it is in *Sodome et Gomorrhe II* (the last volume to appear during Proust's lifetime) that the young peasant from Lozère is both faithfully painted and disguised.

There, her native village, Auxillac, and her family home are described with careful attention to the real-life details, as is the strong character of this young lady of La Canourgue, a goddess from the center of France, 'as open as a lake, but boiling up repeatedly with a fury which recalled the threat of floods and whirlpools that suck down everything, lay waste to everything.' The portraitist doesn't flatter her (she is ignorant, uneducated, insolent) but he extols 'Céleste's strange genius.'

She is a sylph in appearance only. While a certain Nissim Bernard ventures into the cellars of the Grand Hôtel de Balbec in pursuit of young waiters, the narrator climbs up to the top floor to join the chambermaids of an elderly foreign lady. Under the eaves, we find Céleste with her sister, who still bears her maiden name: Marie Gineste. Their admirer feels the need to emphasize, with disconcerting precision, that he is linked to these two 'lady messengers,' as he calls them, by 'very close though very pure friendship.'

The stage is set: the world is turned upside-down. In fact, a carnival scene ensues. As the Céleste in the novel so aptly remarks, less blind than her real-world twin: 'You never can tell what might exist in a life.'

As though she had stepped out of the Comtesse de Ségur's stories, Céleste rifles through drawers, digs up old photographs, talks loudly, makes fun of Monsieur, to whom she gives the names of birds and whom she calls a snake, a night owl, a squirrel, a little black devil, a rogue – and even 'Molière'! The servant takes her revenge on the master. As for Monsieur, the more the cajolers dance around his bed, where he endlessly consumes milk and croissants, the more his self-portrait sheds its mask, mocking through the intermediary of the young ladies his princely airs, his manias, his perfidy, his image of cuddly stuffed animal, with claws.

A séance is brewing: 'As they talked of a stranger who was in the hotel, repeating his words, Céleste and Marie painted his face onto their faces, their mouths became his mouth, their eyes his eyes.'

Those who 'will never read books, nor write them either,' the two maids employed as lady's companions, are put in charge of molding the mortuary mask of this stranger, who is the author himself. Aren't their faces sculpted from the clay of their rivers, haven't they retained the primitive instinct of mimicry?

When she returns all alone, in *La Prisonnière*, Céleste is sweetness itself, goodness incarnate. The narrator has her repeat twice, almost exactly, the same words: 'Divinity or heavenly majesty set down on a bed!' Then he questions her, he needs an interpretation, which applies to both passages: 'Ah,' she responds the first time, 'because you don't resemble anybody in the world. You don't look anything like a man lying down, you aren't in the bed, you don't move a muscle, angels seem to have descended to place you here.'

Lost in revising his text, it would seem that Proust never tires of hearing the tender words of his young girl in flower: 'You have come to lie down here. In this moment, your pure white pajamas and the movements of your neck give you the look of a dove.' Thanks to the other Céleste, Proust plummets into hell, then takes wing toward his little cloud.

Day and Night

For many years now, he has avoided the fresh air. Proust first became a recluse to protect himself against it, secluded, sequestered, kept *at room temperature.* Condemned ever since his youth to flee every aspect of life outdoors, he who adored the country and the sea, he set out for Cabourg one spring day *in a closed car,* to go and 'smell' the hawthorns on the other side of the glass. It is out of the question to do housework or air the rooms as long as he is present. Never are the windows open, nor the carpets beaten. The hustle and bustle starts as soon as he leaves. The servants, it is said, have adopted his quirks; they too sleep during the day. Rumor has it he pays workmen a fortune to hammer their nails in silence.

Although he cannot endure pollen, his bedroom is a greenhouse. His book, a plant. A monstrous plant that never stops growing, as he prunes, grafts, takes cuttings. A night-growing plant, for it tolerates only artificial light. The sun has become his personal enemy: he breathes only when the electric lights come on, when day is over, when night arrives, when Paris falls asleep.

Only at twilight does he begin to live. He is permanently on the wrong side of the law of nature. To him, night is day, and day is night.

If he speaks of 'evening,' it must be understood as six or seven in the morning. He waits until dawn to go to bed. But does he ever go to sleep? He lives backwards, he has destroyed the instinct for slumber. When he needs to knock himself out, he takes trional or veronal. His coffee comes exclusively from Chez Corcellet, on Rue Lévis in the XVIIe arrondissement, to ensure that it is fresh. The coffee pot is kept on, waiting for him. For years caffeine has kept him artificially awake, it has plunged him into a state of perpetual jet lag. With every fiber, he struggles against the pitch-dark, he throws up obstacles in its path, he invents excuses. Back home, he puts on his overcoat to get to work, to descend into himself.

Pierrot

Did his front hall smell of warm bread, brioches, butter croissants? At Rue Hamelin, there is a bakery downstairs.

Is it in light of this proximity that we must seek to understand the response Proust gives, in the game of 'professions,' when he is asked the momentous, nearly posthumous question: 'What manual profession would you have liked to practice?' (The journalists at *L'Intransigeant* loved to solicit his contributions.) 'But I write!' he evidently exclaims, before mentioning one of the less unmentionable manual professions, like an adolescent wishing to reassure his family: 'If the supply of paper ever ran dry,' he concedes to his pursuers: 'baker.'

The interviewee is undoubtedly laughing up his sleeve, just imagining the picture: his portrait as a baker. Of course he would have loved it if his books sold 'like hot cakes'; it's the same success he wishes for the journal Céleste will never write.

But hasn't he in fact become that galley slave who works at night, while the city is resting and renewing its strength? Hasn't this pallid man been floury white for years now? A sorrowful clown like the eternal dandy from whom he never separated himself, the *Pierrot Lunaire*, the high-society Pierrot whom, when he turned twenty-one, Jacques-Émile Blanche had painted in his place, in place of Dorian Gray: an oval portrait of a young man with a camellia, enhanced with a few touches of rouge on the cheeks, the lips.

Doesn't this cloud of flour floating in the room have the same consistency as the dust of time, which submerges everything?

Replacement

It is on the ground floor, in the shop, that the maid can make her *'téléphonages'* in her master's place. She reels off his lines, which she knows by heart; she is his tape recorder. More than once, people have confused her voice on the telephone for his, some becoming angry at having taken Céleste for Monsieur Proust himself.

She is his voice (she reads to him too), she is his eyes (she goes to try out new eyeglasses in his place, he does not have the time), she is his legs (he sends her as his messenger, his ambassador). She is his wings, she is his life (although these days she lives only for him). She is his last link to the daylight.

She is the one who goes for him, for both of them, to look at apartments they might move to. She alone must have been aware that the fifth-floor balcony on Rue Hamelin faces the Eiffel Tower, that the gigantic tower rises into the sky on the other side of his closed shutters, that frontier which he will never cross.

The Invisible Man

If he could have been the invisible man, he would have. He cannot bear to be seen. He wishes he could walk through walls: he dreams of infinite entrances, of causing hidden doors to open to him, of ransacking drawers, cracking safes, knowing the most well-guarded secrets.

He wants to know the password that will let him slip in among conspirators, admit him to the clan, the gang, allow him to be incognito everywhere. He is a marvel at camouflage. He would like to watch everything through one-way mirrors. He is wildly passionate about backstage drama.

He is daring. He is prepared to disguise himself as a girl. He writes to the young Albert Nahmias, who had done everything in his power to help him: 'If only I could change my sex, my face and age, to take on the look of a lovely young woman, to kiss you with all my heart.'

Certain days, certain nights, he rescues virgins with cheeks like peonies. He spares them the worst, he dreams of unconsummated marriages. (Céleste, whom he lodges in his bachelor's quarters, in the maid's room at the end of the corridor, will fulfill this wish – she even has the advantage of being married, married to an absent husband, always busy, off to war, in his car.) If Marcel were rich and healthy enough, he would marry one of his fantasy maidens, never touching her, simply watching her live, receive visitors, give parties, go horseback riding, hold court. Artist and benefactor, he would make it possible for an existence to blossom, as if he were the hero of a Paul Bourget novel. But how could he ever have been satisfied with only one fiancée to englobe beneath a glass bell jar?

He is a jealous lover: he always wants to know what he's not being told, and if you remain silent, this is proof that his suspicion is justified, that something is being hidden from him. But there are rumors about him as well. The best informed, the most malicious go so far as to tell stories about starving rats, scenes of butchery. To the exquisite Antoinette Faure, who in a game of Truth asked him for what fault he would have been the most indulgent, he long ago replied, 'For the private life of geniuses.'

'Let us never discuss our tastes with others, and even less our intimate tastes,' he tells his army of confidants. He loves mystery, secrets. He always has something to hide. 'Don't tell anyone,' he says, to all and sundry. 'Silent as the grave!' he will later add to his vocabulary, in the encrypted language he speaks with his dearest friends. Mum's the word!

Expeditions

The *world* is like a distant land he tried to penetrate. Céleste's husband, who is a taxi driver, puts his vehicle at Proust's disposal at night. No questions asked, he drives him anywhere he pleases (one day they ventured near Rueil, where they were mistaken for confederates of Bonnot's gang).

He goes to plunder the salons, he moves through the great houses as though on a foreign expedition: the Princess de Polignac's, the Princess Soutzo's, Madame Hennessy's.

He needs blood, fresh blood.

High society, Parisian dinners, costume balls are more than simply painted canvases or theater sets. He calls them 'great massacres.' Here are the models he gets to pose for him without their knowledge, here are the muses that inspire him, the ones that madden him, and the guinea pigs on whom he tests out his hypotheses, his fantasies. He verifies. To know for sure, he is prepared to wake up children in the middle of the night. Céleste assures us all it took was his sudden wish to see this person or that for her to know how far along he was in his chapters, 'just as I could have told you, from the way he eliminated someone from his visits, his outings or his letters: "Well, *those* pages are finished."'

He plays checkers with valets, he attracts swarms

of elevator operators, telegraphers, sales clerks, delivery boys, bellboys. He bribes head waiters, who are devoted to him, he weaves a network of spies in mansions and brothels alike. He spreads flattery, tips and smiles among domestic servants, lady's maids. He always succeeds in worming information out of them.

When Proust repeats to Céleste the 'dirt' he has picked up in the Rue de l'Arcade, the vices of others to avoid confessing his own, she grows faint. She is an innocent, like that ancestor of Laure de Chevigné who was so much to the taste of the Marquis de Sade. 'It's not possible, Sir! That can't be!' she stammers. The beautiful, cherubic girl does not understand how her master could have watched 'that.' He responds, 'Precisely, Céleste, because you couldn't make it up.'

For a long time, he has been dragging skeletons into his bedroom. He hides them beneath his bed. Otherwise, why store so much debris in the condemned rooms of his castle, why all these remains, these relics, these criminal exhibits?

Unfathomed Depths

He isn't content just to investigate, he in no way resembles the professional observer, he is not (not only) an herbalist or entomologist. He is irrepressibly attracted by strong sensations, murky backgrounds, vertiginous perspectives and unfathomed depths alike. He must walk into the lion's den.

He wanders the slopes of Vesuvius. *Tableaux vivants*, when they are finally revealed as what they should be, what they should never stop being – miniature visions of hell – delight him. With his eyes, he can touch them.

'You can feel the abyss he opens up,' says Jacques Rivière, 'and how discreetly!' 'He lived vicariously through you, admired you, loved you, took part in your foibles and your vices… He devoured everything he could find in the time he spent on you.' What François Mauriac sums up here is formulated more bluntly by his friend Jacques Porel: 'No author has been at once more ferocious and more compassionate toward his characters. He turns them inside out like rabbit skins, but first he falls madly in love with them. Then suddenly, beneath his pen, these wretched creatures take on enormous importance. It is as though they were being championed by a great admirer.'

Last Outings

Toward the end, his outings dwindle. They elate but, increasingly, 'kill' him: the exhibition of Dutch painting at the Jeu de Paume, where he goes – one *morning*! – to contemplate Vermeer's little patch of yellow wall, the infinity at the heart of the color, before moving on to admire Ingres next, as though it were vital that he be enveloped, sated one last time by rounded flesh and perfect forms.

And then several evenings like those of the old days, once at the Schiffs' after the opera with Igor Stravinsky, Serge de Diaghilev, Pablo Picasso, James Joyce (who thought he looked younger than his age). He went to two or three grand dinners, the last like a farewell at the Count and Countess de Beaumont's, at the beginning of October.

He scarcely sees his friends anymore. Years ago he canceled his telephone subscription so as not to be disturbed. One evening, one night, he convened the musicians of the Poulet Quartet at Rue Hamelin. For him, for him alone, they play César Franck.

Incorporeal

He does not eat anymore, then suddenly he has the cravings of a pregnant woman, he must have a filet of sole, sometimes mullet, French fries, Olivier salad, or petits fours – but they must be from Chez Rebattet.

He takes inordinate care of his body, like an ascetic, like an athlete (at twenty-five, this delicate man had actually fought a duel against Jean Lorrain, who had dared to call him effeminate, and he dreamt of doing it again). The fragrances of soap and eau de Cologne, like all other scents, were anathema to him. Despite the absence of running water, he is obsessive about his personal hygiene. He never shaves himself, but he refuses to appear in public looking unkempt, much less in front of ladies, with a two- or three-day beard. He has always feared scented letters; eventually, he even has a special mailbox and disinfects the mail that he receives with formalin. He wears gloves in bed for fear of germs.

This man so careful of his appearance is literally packed in layers of wool, wrapped up, swaddled in undershirts. Still lying in his bed, his head scarcely raised, he has already put on a pajama top over his old wool sweaters. He always has supplies on hand, just in case.

Céleste has to warm up his clothes in the oven, at

the risk of scorching them. He has had a curtain nailed over the bedroom door to keep out drafts. He is perpetually cold — to such a degree that during the heat wave which struck down Paris in July of 1921, as he confesses to a correspondent, he worked on his book 'under seven wool blankets and a fur throw, with three hot water bottles and a fire going.'

He spends a fortune on medications. The best remedy he has yet found to bring down a persistent fever, on certain nights, is to send his chauffeur to the Ritz Bar for carafes of beer, which he likes to drink iced. The coffee with milk that ultimately becomes his only form of nourishment gives his skin a unique pallor, like ivory.

The Mist of Fumigations

His bedroom is plunged in a mist of fumigations; he has the powders kept burning in saucers. He never uses matches, because of the smell of sulfur. Instead, he lights pieces of paper with the candle flame that must be kept burning night and day in the little hall next door – his candles are bought in five-kilo boxes, near the Saint-Lazare railroad station.

Céleste has never in her life forgotten the first time she entered the bedroom. It was already like a goodbye: 'Of Monsieur Proust I could make out only the white shirt beneath a heavy sweater and his upper body propped up with two pillows. His face was lost in shadow and the fog of fumigation, completely invisible except for the eyes, which looked at me – I felt them more than I saw them.'

Is he training to play dead, he who holds his breath and does not move a muscle when the servant, at his bidding, comes into the room? Take a good look at him. Quite suddenly he stops talking to the visitor he is receiving and closes his eyes: 'I need rest,' he announces simply. And he is gone, although continuing to speak – as if some other half of himself were picking up the conversation in his place.

In time, it was inevitable that the puppet master – with his famous scientific and philosophical puppet show – would metamorphose into a puppet himself. He is a mannequin that must be carried around, dressed, manipulated. You'd think he were stuffed.

When had he stopped living, or was he only pretending?

But if one lives the life of a writer, does one still truly belong to the human species?

This peculiar being, this 'one of a kind' about whom all of us say to ourselves, when reading his work: 'That's me!' – his sole nourishment, his sole instrument, is language, subjects, verbs, objects, sentences, adjectives, adverbs, prepositions, conjunctions, tenses, all that is unique to man, and nothing else.

Untouchable

Surely he must know everything, as do the dead who observe us, the spirits in the other world from whom we can hide nothing.

He is not a man; he is a simulacrum. If he were really human, why would he disguise himself as a rag doll, why would he have the flimsiness of a child's toy slipped beneath the pillow? Why does he feast on images that he brings home with him, on bodies of shiny paper, why does he prefer distant voices, like the sirens heard through the receiver of the Theatrophone?

Is he even flesh, when he can no longer tolerate solid food? Does he really have skin? His body is washed with the lightest of touches, aided by an unbelievable number of towels, as though he feared the colors of his face, the red of his lips might rub off, feared the erasure of the last trace of life. The erasure of himself.

Although fascinated by the other, other bodies cause him boundless panic. When he has tamed this fear, when he can no longer make anything out of this passion, when this is no longer his raw material, his living material, but the black thing he sees advancing toward his deathbed, the enormous thing that wishes to annihilate him, he no longer has any reason to resist, he has to leave.

Living or dying, nobody can touch him. But has

anybody, since childhood, been able to touch him? Marcel Proust passes away after getting an injection. He had forbidden injections. He knew very well that he would immediately fall to dust, that this pinch would exile him forever from his dream.

Tomorrow

Toward midnight, that evening, he rings the bell, he calls. Céleste is waiting in the room next door. She is there all the time, every second of every minute. He knows this. It is their pact. She is not like his adored mother, who was always abandoning him and leaving him alone beneath the pink comforter in the little bedroom at the top of the stairs with the red hexagonal tiles, behind the gray cardboard facade of his childhood house.

The young woman with the Mona Lisa smile comes to sit at his feet. Until two in the morning he dictates, he adds details to improve the episode of Bergotte's death, the *danse macabre* of the physicians, 'the incredible frivolity of the dying,' a cup of champagne he will never drink, like the brush's final touch on the canvas.

It is terribly cold in the bedroom. Céleste is exhausted, she is dead on her feet, but she stays. He takes over from her, he returns to the third version of *La Prisonnière*, his hand trembles on the typewritten pages, he works until three-thirty in the morning, he reaches page 136, he can't go on, they will continue tomorrow, he dies at approximately five o'clock in the afternoon.

Alive

When he wrote the words 'The End' at the bottom of his manuscript a few weeks earlier, in spring, he knew perfectly well it was an author's phrase, a false conclusion, a *happy end,* as Odette would have said, or Madame Verdurin. A *coup de théâtre* (to tell Céleste, to speak to her *on waking:* he hadn't done that for ages!), a ruse engineered to put her off the scent, for she was only too happy to take him at his word (afterwards, they were going to change their lives, they'd paint the town red, he promised a trip around the world, a bohemian existence, a palatial sanatorium in fields of snow).

He had written the phrase 'The End' as one might glimpse the Promised Land, but he knew perfectly well that it was necessary to continue, nothing was finished, the work should remain imperfect, he would not see its last words, he would die before it did, the work would keep him, to the very end, alive.

BOOKSHELF

Apart from Céleste Albaret's exceptional memories, collected by Georges Belmont under the title *Monsieur Proust* (Robert Laffont, 1973; New York Review Books Classics, 2003), the details of Proust's life come essentially from works by those who knew Proust. Notably:

The *Hommage à Marcel Proust* in the January 1923 issue of *La Nouvelle Revue française* (contributors include Anna de Noailles, Robert Proust, Robert Dreyfus, Reynaldo Hahn, Fernand Gregh, Gaston Gallimard, Lucien Daudet, Jacques-Émile Blanche, Georges de Lauris, Philippe Soupault, Gabriel de la Rochefoucauld, Walter Berry, Jean Cocteau, Paul Morand, Jacques Porel, Ramon Fernandez, Jacques Rivière, etc); and, in no particular order, the first volume of *Poésie critique* by Jean Cocteau, (Gallimard, 1959); as well as that of *Les Mémorables* by Maurice Martin du Gard (Flammarion, 1957); *Journal d'un attaché d'ambassade, 1916–1917* by Paul Morand (Gallimard, 1996); *Souvenirs d'un collectionneur* by René Gimpel (Calmann-Lévy, 1963); *Mon ami Marcel Proust* by Maurice Duplay (Cahiers Marcel Proust, Gallimard, 1972), *Mon amitié avec Marcel Proust* by Fernand Gregh (Grasset, 1958); *Avec Marcel Proust* by Marcel Plantevignes (Nizet, 1966); *Le Regard de la mémoire* by Jean Hugo (Actes Sud, 1983); *Fils de Réjane* by Jacques Porel (Plon, 1951); *Au bal avec Marcel Proust* by Princess Bibesco (Gallimard, 1928); *Suite familière* by Léon-Paul Fargue (Émile-Paul, 1928); *Autour de soixante lettres de Marcel Proust* by Lucien Daudet (Gallimard, 1929); *Souvenirs des milieux littéraires* by Léon Daudet (Robert Laffont, 1992); *Du côté de chez Proust* by François Mauriac (La Table ronde, 1947); *Sylvia* and *Présence des morts* by Emmanuel Berl (Gallimard, 1952 et 1956); *Souvenirs sur Marcel Proust* (Grasset, 1926) and *De Monsieur Thiers à Marcel Proust* by Robert Dreyfus (Plon 1939); *Mes modèles* by Jacques-Émile Blanche (Stock,1928), *Notes: Journal d'un musicien* by Reynaldo Hahn (Plon, 1933); *Pays parisiens* by Daniel Halévy (Grasset, 1932) and his correspondance with Proust (éditions de Fallois, 1992); *Marcel Proust* by Léon Pierre-Quint (Le Sagittaire, 1935), *Le Sabbat* by Maurice Sachs (Corréa, 1946), the brief 'Mémoires d'un valet de chambre' by Ernest Forssgren (*Cahiers Marcel Proust n° 7*, Gallimard 1975). To these must be added: *Proust et Céleste* by Christian Péchenard (La Table ronde, 1996), *Le Paris de Marcel Proust* by Isabelle Ottaviani and Philippe Poulain (Paris Musées, 1996); the biography of Ghislain de Diesbach (Perrin, 1990); the major *Marcel Proust* by Jean-Yves Tadié (Gallimard, 1996) and the correspondance edited by Philippe Kolb (Plon 1970–1993).

ACKNOWLEDGMENTS

My thanks to Françoise Dumas, Dominique Janvier, Gérard Macé, Raoul Ruiz and Thierry Thomas, each of whom, in one way or another, inspired this book, as well as to Nancy Kline for her enthusiasm and perseverance, and to Anne-Solange Noble, Colette Fellous and Jean Frémon for their support. – JP

Many thanks to my faithful readers Michael Carman, Sally Fisher, Vicki Hallerman and Susan Sindall; my ad hoc rhymers Neil Blackadder, Kasey Jueds and Natania Rosenfeld; and my meticulous editors Cécile Lee and Clem Clement. My warmest gratitude to Jérôme Prieur for entrusting me with his wit and erudition in these pages. – NK

Jérôme Prieur is a writer and filmmaker. He holds PhDs in law and literature, the latter supervised by Hélène Cixous. His books and films bear witness to an obsession with traces of the past, images, archives, and the presence of the departed. He is the author of around twenty books, including *Roman noir*, on Gothic literature (notably, *The Private Memoirs and Confession of a Justified Sinner* by James Hogg); *Rendez-vous dans une autre vie*, in search of the ghosts of Pompeii and of the 1900 Paris Exposition; *La moustache du soldat inconnu*, in which he claims to relate 'his memories of the Great War'; and recently *Regarder et ne pas voir*, a chiaroscuro portrait of a witness to the events of the 1930s and '40s. In his latest, multi-award-winning film, *Sentinels of Forgetting*, the protagonists are the sculpted figures on memorials of the First World War.

Nancy Kline grew up in Greenwich Village (NYC). Her essays, short stories, memoirs and reviews have appeared widely in the USA. She has published more than ten books, which include fiction, literary criticism, biography, and translations of René Char, Paul Éluard, Lorand Gaspar, Claudine Herrmann, and Jules Supervielle. She reviews for the *New York Times* and has taught at Harvard, UCLA, and Barnard College of Columbia University, where she founded the Writing Program. She is currently on the faculty of the Bard Prison Initiative.

Also published by Les Fugitives

In 'the quick brown fox' collection:

Harriet Armstrong
To Rest Our Minds and Bodies

Erica van Horn
We Still Have the Telephone

Charlotte Beeston
The White Flower

Michèle Roberts
French Cooking for One

Penelope Curtis
After Nora

Kyra Wilder
Gloss

Lauren Elkin
No. 91/92: notes on a Parisian commute

In translation from French:

Catherine Axelrad
Célina
trans. Philip Terry

Mireille Gansel
Translation as Transhumance
trans. Ros Schwartz

Jeanne Benameur
The Child Who
trans. Bill Johnston

Maylis de Kerangal
Eastbound
trans. Jessica Moore

Ananda Devi
Eve out of Her Ruins
The Living Days
trans. Jeffrey Zuckerman

Julia Kerninon
A Respectable Occupation
trans. Ruth Diver

Camille Laurens
Little Dancer Aged Fourteen
trans. Willard Wood

Colette Fellous
This Tilting World
trans. Sophie Lewis

Noémi Lefebvre
Blue Self-Portrait
Poetics of Work
trans. Sophie Lewis

Jean Frémon
Now, Now, Louison;
Nativity, trans. Cole Swensen
Portrait Tales, trans. John Taylor

Nathalie Léger
Suite for Barbara Loden
trans. Natasha Lehrer
Exposition
trans. Amanda DeMarco
The White Dress
trans. Natasha Lehrer

Emilienne Malfatto
May the Tigris Grieve for You
trans. Lorna Scott Fox

Lucie Paye
Absence
trans. Natasha Lehrer

Shumona Sinha
Down with the Poor!
trans. Teresa Lavender Fagan

Clara Schulmann
Chicanes, trans. Clem Clement,
Ruth Diver, Lauren Elkin, et al.

Anne Serre
The Governesses;
The Fool and Other Moral Tales
trans. Mark Hutchinson

Sylvie Weil
Selfies
trans. Ros Schwartz